─GREAT WALKS─
PEAK DISTRICT

GREAT WALKS

PEAK DISTRICT

JOHN AND ANNE NUTTALL
Photography by John Heseltine
Series Editor Frank Duerden

This special edition has been
produced in 1992
by New Orchard Editions Ltd,
Villiers House, 41/47 Strand,
London WC2N 5JE,
a Cassell company
for publication
by Printwise Publications Ltd,
47 Bradshaw Road Tottington,
Bury, Lancs BL8 3PW

Photography by John Heseltine

Printed and bound in Spain by Graficromo S.A.

ISBN 1-87222632-9

Half title page *Rocks on Kinder Plateau*

Title page *Eyam Edge looking west from Bretton*

CONTENTS

ACKNOWLEDGMENTS

We want to record our appreciation of the many people who have helped us during the writing of this book.

First of all thank you to Roland Smith and Andrew Greenwood of the Peak Park Board who checked the manuscript.

During the walks we met and talked with many of the full-time and part-time Peak District rangers. Mr Geoff Frost, Mr Brian Jones, Mr Tony Hood, Mrs Margaret Bailey, and their colleagues were very informative and most helpful.

We would also like to thank Mr Peter Gray, the Chairman of the Derbyshire and Lancashire Gliding Club; Mr Dave Wilson of the National Trust, who checked our list of routes; Mr A.F. Roberts and Mr J.R. Leach, authors of *The Coal Mines of Buxton*; and Alan and Hilda Mitchell for their help on the section on farming.

We thank the following for permission to use material from their publications: The Peak Park Joint Planning Board ('Access to Open Country') and the Countryside Commission ('The Countryside Access Charter'). The maps were drawn from the Outdoor Leisure and Pathfinder maps of the area with the permission of the Ordnance Survey.

Thank you also to our two sons, Jeremy and Joseph, who have put up with their parents' obsession.

Finally thank you to Mark Richards who gave us the opportunity of writing this book. We've enjoyed every minute of it.

INTRODUCTION

During the writing of this book we have visited and revisited many familiar parts of the Peak District. Yet every time there is something new to see, to hear and to experience. Whether it has been wandering along Stanage Edge under a cloudless blue sky, or returning by moonlight down Alport Dale or even groping our way by compass off Bleaklow in mist and rain, we have enjoyed it all.

In an area with so much to offer, the choice of the best walks is never easy as it always means leaving something out. After much deliberation there were still places which we wanted to include and there was always the temptation to make every walk just that little bit longer to get something special in; but in the end, in our opinion, this selection gives the finest of the Peak District walks. They vary considerably in length and difficulty, so there should be something to suit everyone's inclination and the time available. The shortest walks are in general the easiest, but what may present no problems for one person can be an insuperable obstacle for another, so any grading system is bound to be subjective. Each walk has a route description followed by information on things to see along the way, but the book begins with a description of the Peak District as a whole, covering such subjects as the formation of peat, the ubiquitous red grouse, rock climbing and farming.

John Heseltine has captured the spirit and special quality of the Peak District in his excellent photographs. These will give a great deal of pleasure and bring back many happy memories for us.

The White Peak and the Dark Peak cover a fascinating area which is within only a few miles of nearly half the population of England. Sometimes, close to Sheffield on a sunny Sunday, it can indeed be crowded; yet on many occasions we have walked for hours without meeting another person. To lie on your back in the heather or bilberries on Bleaklow with only the call of the lark in the sky above is to be really content. But it is not always good weather! The wild moors can be very wild indeed and in bad weather to the unwary or ill prepared they can be savage and unforgiving of a mistake. It is a long way down from Bleaklow or Black Hill and in freezing rain, with night fast approaching, it can seem to take forever. Every year the Mountain Rescue teams are called out many times to search for missing or injured walkers.

However, even though warm sun and blue skies make

excellent weather for walking, the less good conditions are often just as enjoyable and sometimes far more memorable. In winter Kinder Downfall can freeze to a magnificent sheet of ice, while heavy snowfall delights the skiers. Even in thick cloud there is considerable satisfaction in navigating your way through the mist to see the trig point materialize just where you had expected it to be. Above all, to be on the high moors when the sun breaks through the swirling clouds, or to climb out of the valley mist to find the tops clear and the valley bottom filled with white rivers of fog, or to crunch your way over the iron-hard, frozen peat, these are the moments that will live for ever.

THE PEAK DISTRICT NATIONAL PARK

National Parks are areas of country with exceptionally attractive scenery that are specially protected. Britain was not the first country to introduce National Parks; the Yellowstone National Park in America, established as long ago as 1870, predates the Peak Park by eighty years.

The purpose of a National Park is to protect the more attractive parts of the country from being spoilt and to set aside areas for people who live in towns and cities to enjoy open air recreation. In Britain the title National Park is misleading as it is not a park in the urban sense, neither is it owned by the nation. The Parks, unlike many National Parks abroad, are not undeveloped wildernesses. The Peak Park, although sparsely inhabited in comparison with the surrounding heartland of industrial Britain, is home to many people and its 'unspoilt' scenery owes much to the activity of man. Most of the land in fact belongs to private farmers and landowners. Although much of Britain is under private ownership, which makes public access difficult, in the National Parks there is generally freer access to open country than elsewhere, either by custom, as in the Lake District, or by formal Access Agreements with the landowners. The latter covers large areas of Peak District open moorland.

In 1935 the Council for the Preservation of Rural England set up a Standing Committee for National Parks. The National Parks and Access to the Countryside Act of 1949 was responsible for the creation of each individual Park in England and Wales. Ten National Parks have so far been established. The Countryside Commission took over responsibility for the Parks in 1968 and, in 1974, an administrative authority was set up in each Park.

The National Park Authorities are responsible for conservation, the control of development and the provision of facilities for visitors. They try to combine support for the local economy with conservation and provision for recreation.

Since 1974 the Peak District National Park has been managed by a Joint Planning Board. This has a technical department at Bakewell and devotes its attention to the special problems of the Peak District. It has 34 members, of whom 23 are appointed by the County and District Councils having territory in the National Park, and 11 by the Secretary of State for the

Opposite Rocks near Crowden Tower

Environment, who are chosen for their special knowledge of some aspect of the work of the Park.

Peak Park Information Centres which advise and help visitors are at:

Bakewell; Old Market Hall (Bakewell 3227)
Castleton; Castle Street (Hope Valley 20679)
Edale; Fieldhead (Hope Valley 70207)
Fairholmes; Upper Derwent Valley
Torside; Longdendale Valley
Hartington; Hartington Old Station

The opening times of the information centres vary, some are not open in the winter.

SOME FACTS AND FIGURES ABOUT THE PEAK DISTRICT NATIONAL PARK

DESIGNATED Designation confirmed in April 1951. The Peak District was the first National Park in Great Britain.

AREA 542 sq miles (140 400 hectares). This covers a large amount of Derbyshire plus adjoining parts of Staffordshire, Cheshire, Greater Manchester, and West and South Yorkshire. The greatest length north to south is nearly 40 miles (65 km), and the greatest breadth about 24 miles (39 km). The long central slice of land excluded from the park is industrial and includes the towns of New Mills, Whaley Bridge, Chapel en le Frith and Buxton. The latter has extensive limestone quarries. Matlock and Darley Dale are also omitted.

EMBLEM A locally quarried millstone. These will be seen beside many of the roads leading into the park.

POPULATION Nearly 40 000 people live and work in the area of the Park. The principal town is Bakewell with about 4 000 inhabitants.

TOURISTS About 17 million people live within 60 miles (95 km) of its boundary. The Park can be approached from all directions and is frequented at all times of the year by people from the nearby industrial centres. Around 20 million day visitors come each year.

FINANCE This is derived mainly from the government with a smaller sum from the ratepayers, each one of whom pays less than the cost of a first class stamp in support for all ten Parks. The Park earns 30% of its income through its own activities.

LAND OWNERSHIP Most of the land in the Park is privately owned. Some is owned by public bodies like the water authorities, the National Trust and the National Park Authority, while other areas are specially managed nature reserves.

THE FACE OF THE PEAK DISTRICT

THE GEOLOGY OF THE PEAK DISTRICT

Although this area is called the Peak District there is in fact no single summit. The word 'Peak' comes from the Old English 'Peac' meaning a knoll or hill, and in AD 924 this area was known as 'Peacland'. The wild, high moorland and the black rock of the escarpments in the north contrast with the green dales, chequered fields and silvery rocks further south.

The high moorland in the north of the Peak District rises to just over 2000 ft (610 m) and is composed mainly of millstone grit. This extends down either side of the area forming a horseshoe of gritstone round the central limestone plateau which is 1000–1500 ft (305–460 m) high. The two areas are joined by softer shales and by sandstones which form wide river valleys and gentle hills.

The oldest rock is the limestone, which was formed in the Carboniferous Period 330 million years ago from the shells of sea creatures. There are different textures and colours and the limestone also contains pockets of other rocks; siliceous chert and silica sand were deposited while basalt was formed due to

Between Nether Tor and Upper Tor on Kinder Plateau

volcanic action. Later volcanic action also caused lead and a small amount of copper to be deposited as ores in veins in the limestone. Some of the limestone is very pure and in places it can be up to 2000 ft (610 m) thick.

Shales, grits and sandstones covered the limestone and, in places, vegetation became included which formed coal. Later the whole area was uplifted creating an enormous dome. The upper rocks have since weathered away leaving a central limestone plateau with the younger millstone grit round the edges where it forms rocky escarpments.

In places such as at Castleton, the limestone has been slowly dissolved away by water to form subterranean channels giving dry valleys, caves and underground streams.

THE DARK PEAK

This is the name given to the northern part of the Peak District. The Ordnance Survey Outdoor Leisure maps divide the Peak into two parts, north and south. These are called the Dark Peak and the White Peak, though the land characteristic of the Dark Peak really extends down both the east and west high ground of the southern area.

The Dark Peak is mainly gritstone, composed of bleak featureless moorland, steep rocky edges, isolated weird-shaped sandstone tors, with steep sided cloughs and secret swift-flowing streams. In the winter the whole appearance of the area is one of darkness with dark brown peat hags, black stone walls and forbidding rocky edges, until winter snows transform the moors into a dazzling white wilderness. It is one of the loneliest places in England, in spite of its proximity to large industrial towns. However it has a beauty of its own and can be alive with colour; the gold and yellow of the moorland grass, the purple heather and the white tufts of cotton-sedge grass.

The soil in the Dark Peak is very acid so that there is not a great deal of farming here. The high moorlands are very flat because the bedding planes of the millstone grit are mainly horizontal giving a feeling of spaciousness. It is suitable only for sheep and grouse as the climate is harsh with a high annual rainfall of over 60 in (1520 mm). Over 7 in (180 mm) of rain can fall in a few hours even in the summer. It snows for about seventy days a year and persistent mist and hill fog on the high moors limit sunshine to less than 1000 hours per year.

The vegetation of the Dark Peak is composed of cotton grass on the high moors with matt grass and purple moor grass. There is also ling and bracken on well-drained ground. These together with the gritstone give the Dark Peak its characteristic appearance. Besides the grouse and sheep, the only other creatures to be found are the curlew, the golden plover, the fox and the mountain hare. The hare, which exchanges a brown summer coat for a white one in the winter, is at the southernmost limit of its territory. The cloudberry, which has a flower similar to the blackberry and a red edible fruit, is also found no further south.

Man has very significantly influenced the landscape. By felling the trees and introducing grazing animals the regeneration of woodland has been prevented. Valleys have been flooded to form reservoirs and hillsides have been planted with conifers. At intervals the heather is burned to promote the growth of young shoots for the grouse and sheep.

Although the area is crossed by three major trunk roads, the bleakness of the moors makes the small village communities in the valleys even more attractive. These are mostly self contained and based on hill farming.

THE WHITE PEAK

This is the limestone heart of the Peak District and is much less wild than the Dark Peak. The climate is milder, with only 35–40 in (890–1020 mm) of rain each year, but as much of the land is between 1000–1500 ft (305–460 m) it can still be very bleak in the winter.

The landscape really is white, the main feature being the gleaming miles of limestone walls that undulate over the green hills and valleys. The hills are mostly low with clumps of trees on the top. In places the rivers have cut down through the limestone to form steep-sided dales with caves, cliffs and pinnacles. Sometimes the rivers go underground and most of the smaller dales are dry.

The countryside is much softer and more fertile than the Dark Peak. The soil is light and gives good pastures and hence the hand of man is evident everywhere. Most of the farming is dairy and there is little arable land, while the sturdy farm buildings and white stone villages, which are characteristic of the area, form an attractive complement to the pastoral scene.

The flora of the limestone country is much more varied than that of the gritstone. It is closer to that of the more southern parts of Britain and is the northern boundary of the habitats of some plants and animals.

The limestone area is very small and is under great pressure from quarrying interests as the rock is much in demand as a basic ingredient for cement and also for road making. This produces a conflict in the use of the White Peak as although part of it is heavily industrialized (the Peak District has twelve limestone quarries, all with an active life still to run of around twenty years), it is also a very beautiful area with demands on it for recreation.

FARMING IN THE PEAK DISTRICT

Farming is the most important and the largest single industry in the Peak District. The farms are small, mainly owner-occupied, and are usually based on grass and hill farming. About three-quarters of them have less than 75 acres (30 hectares) and two-thirds less than 50 acres (20 hectares) of land.

EARLY FARMING

The Peak District has been farmed for many hundreds of years. The earliest signs of cultivation can be seen as lines of undulations in the fields known as lynchets.

By the Middle Ages the open field system of agriculture had been developed in the limestone part of the Peak, although the gritstone areas were still mainly wooded. The arable land near to a village was divided up into two or three large fields, which were subdivided into strips, and each strip would be farmed by a different person. The long, parallel, walled fields are also part of the early enclosure system probably used for stock farming. Each village had its own pinfold or walled enclosure where stray beasts were impounded, and some of these remain to this day.

A large proportion of the land remained open however, until the Enclosure Acts of 1760–1830 when the landscape of the Peak District was transformed in a very short period of time. Long, regular walls appeared in geometric patterns all over the countryside, each built to exact standards of height, width and slope, with even the number of through stones to be included stipulated by the commissioners. Many new farms and roads were built, thus altering the whole appearance of the landscape.

Dewponds are a feature of the limestone area. These are shallow, circular depressions which were constructed for the stock to drink from. They are filled by rain water and often had a road water drain emptying into them.

SHEEP FARMING

This is the traditional type of farming in hill country and the number of sheep farmed increased rapidly after the Enclosure Acts.

The oldest breed of sheep farmed is the Woodland White Faced. This came originally from Hope Woodlands. The sheep have white faces and long white legs, and both the rams and ewes are horned. At one time they were kept for their wool, but they are now a rare breed. They have a strong hefting or homing instinct. There is a story that 150 years ago a flock was sold to a farmer in Kent; two of the sheep did not settle and eventually made their way back home, a distance of some 200 miles (320 km).

The most common breed before the Enclosure Acts was the Old Limestone. These sheep have a long body, are very heavy and bony, with a thick skin and coarse wool.

These two breeds, the Woodland White Faced and the Old Limestone, were probably crossed to form the Derbyshire Gritstone, which is now the most popular breed of sheep in the Dark Peak. It is very hardy, has a speckled face and legs and no horns. It was first shown at Bakewell in 1906.

Two other popular breeds in the hill country are the Swaledale and the Lonk. The latter is a large hill breed with a dense fleece which dries quickly. It is a very self-sufficient sheep, and it has to be as it spends much of its life on the desolate moors. It has an evenly black-and-white face and is horned. The Swaledale is horned with a black face and grey muzzle. Many hill farmers cross half breed Swaledale and Gritstone ewes with a Suffolk ram; the lambs are then sold for meat.

Jacobs sheep can now be seen quite often. This was once a rare breed, but has now become commercially established. The wool is much in demand for spinning.

The main breeds kept on the lower uplands are Clun Forest, which is a fat horned sheep with curly wool round a black face, and Suffolk, a fat sheep with a narrow black face without horns, which is not as hardy.

In the past sheep were always washed before shearing, and each village had a special place, sometimes a bridge, for doing this. This practice has now been discontinued as it washes the grease out of the fleece.

'A bonfire turnout gives an April Fool lamb': on the hill farms the ram is put with the ewes in November. The sheep are then given extra feed over the winter and brought down to the farms to lamb in March/April. Some hill farmers over-winter their sheep in Cheshire and these are usually put to lamb in a shed. As soon as the lambs are strong enough they go back onto the hills until the sheep are brought down again for shearing and dipping in June, and again for the lambs to be sold round about October.

CATTLE

There has been cattle breeding in the Peak District since the *Domesday Book*. Until 1800 the Longhorn and the Blue Albion breeds of oxen were used for draught purposes. Dairy products were produced for consumption at home and also sold to supplement the income. At the end of the nineteenth century

Opposite Sheep farming is the traditional type of farming in hill country

many small cheese factories were set up. The Industrial Revolution caused a greater demand for milk in the towns near the Peak District, and as road and rail transport developed, so dairy farming on the limestone and lower parts of the gritstone increased. Much of the land was improved by drainage and reclamation.

The main breed of dairy cow found in the Peak today is the Friesian, which is black and white, while the most common beef bull is the Hereford, brown with a brown-and-white face and the Charollais, which is a pale beige colour. Store cattle are produced by crossing the Friesian with these. Suckler herds of beef cows, often crossbreeds, with the bull running with the cows and calves, are kept by the hill farmer and these are usually sold at the local calf sales in January.

NATIONAL PARK RANGERS

The Peak Park Ranger Service was set up in 1954 and consists of sixteen full-time rangers, supplemented at weekends and holiday periods by many part-time and voluntary workers. Its main role is to help and advise the visitor and to act as the local representative of the Board in dealing with the pressures on the area caused by the large numbers of people. The provision of a ranger service is a legal requirement of an Access Agreement. The rangers maintain contact with the local residents and do much small scale work for conservation and recreation throughout the park. Most are experienced walkers and many are members of mountain rescue teams.

PEAT

Peat is composed mainly of sphagnum moss and forms in poorly-drained areas which have a high annual rainfall. About 7 500 years ago the plateau of Bleaklow and Kinder produced ideal conditions for peat formation and as the climate became wetter, sphagnum bog developed above 1200 ft (370 m). The waterlogging inhibited bacterial activity so that plant remains failed to decompose. The small hollows on the moor were then colonized by sphagnum moss. As one plant died, another grew on top of it, thus accumulating a mass of dead moss to form basin peat. In good conditions the sphagnum moss would then grow outwards to form blanket peat. The lower levels of the plateau remained forested as the climate there was less severe.

Gradually a raised bog developed, higher in the centre than at the edges. When this became waterlogged, it gave way, causing erosion to take place, first of all along the edge, then along channels into the peat. Complex patterns were created, giving the moorland its characteristic form as accumulation and erosion took place at the same time. Deep V-shaped gullies, called groughs, now cut into the peat, which in places is eroded away to the bedrock. The channels get smaller towards the centre of the plateau where they merge with the peat hags of the highest moor. This is known as dendritic patterning and can be seen most clearly from the air.

In places the depth of the peat can be up to 20 ft (6 m). Because of the anaerobic conditions a small number of pollen grains are preserved, maintaining a record of the surrounding plant life for 7000 years. Each pollen grain has an individual shape and pattern by which it can be identified under the microscope, so building up a picture of the vegetation for many miles around. By taking samples of pollen grains from different depths of peat and using radioactive carbon dating techniques, the vegetational history of the locality can be determined.

Although sphagnum moss is the dominant plant in peat, there are few areas of blanket bog left and the moors have been covered for the last two centuries with cotton grass. This vegetation change may have been caused by alteration in the climate, or by the draining and burning of the moors that has taken place since the enclosures of the eighteenth century. However it is most likely to be due to atmospheric pollution following the Industrial Revolution. There are very few lichens on the high moors, and moorland fences show corrosion due to the large amounts of sulphur dioxide in the atmosphere. The cotton grass, being more resistant to the pollution, has become the dominant species. It appears thus that man can unwittingly alter the vegetation of the highest and most inaccessible moors.

RED GROUSE

The high moors of the Dark Peak are the home of the red grouse which is a game bird said to give the best shooting sport in the world. The red grouse has dark, mottled, red-brown plumage with whitish feathered legs and the cock bird has a prominent red wattle over the eyes. It has a typical game bird whirring flight and makes a loud 'go back' cry when startled. The hen lays her eggs in a little scraped out hollow on the ground and in times of danger feigns a broken wing to lure intruders away from the young. The birds feed mainly on heather supplemented by insects. Red grouse are a native bird unique to Britain, and they are found only in northern England, Scotland and Ireland.

There are a large number of shooting cabins on the moors, most of them now in ruins and shooting butts are to be found on most of the high ground. Made of either stone or turf, these hide the guns while the beaters, forming a long line across the moors, drive the birds towards them. The record for killing the most birds in a single day was set up in 1913 when 2843 grouse were shot by nine guns. Very little shooting took place in 1986 as the number of grouse had declined considerably. A test shoot on Ronksley Moor showed that the majority of the grouse being killed were birds less than a year old. This decline may be due to the previous bad winter. Some moors are closed for a few days once a year in the shooting season which starts on the 'Glorious Twelfth' (see page 188).

The presence of the grouse has done much to preserve the high moors. These are managed by a scheme of controlled burning of the heather to give new shoots for the young grouse to eat, while retaining some older plants to form ground cover for nesting.

ROCK CLIMBING

Rock climbing in the Peak District began in the closing years of the nineteenth century and, as Haskett-Smith is forever associated with the ascent of Napes Needle in the Lake District, so in the Peak District the early days are associated with J.W. Puttrell. In 1898 the Climber's Club was born, with J.W.P. as a founder member, and this was followed in 1902 by the Manchester-based Rucksack Club. Most of the early climbing was on the gritstone edges and, although Ilam Rock, that incredible leaning pinnacle in Dovedale, was conquered, limestone was generally considered at this time to be too loose and dangerous for much serious climbing.

Exploration and discovery continued with growing interest up to the outbreak of World War I. Of the names that are associated with the inter-war years, Fred Pigott and Morley Wood stand out. It was they who pioneered many of the climbs on the Roaches, which, although easy by modern standards, are fine climbs and still very popular today. The depression years saw further development of gritstone climbing as men escaped from the oppressive and hopeless cities into the Peak, and increasingly harder routes were explored.

The view north-east from Win Hill

The end of World War II saw an explosion of activity. New equipment, especially nylon rope, helped a further increase in standards. Hemp rope, which had been used until then, will break under the shock of only a short fall; but nylon is elastic and shock absorbing, so that a fall, if properly protected, need not be fatal for the leader. Peter Harding at this time set a new standard with Suicide Wall at Cratcliffe Tor, which was one of the hardest climbs until Joe Brown came on the scene in the late 1940s.

Joe and his companions produced probably the biggest single leap forward in standards, not only in the Peak District, but especially in Wales and in the Alps. Joined by Don Whillans in 1951 with the formation of the Rock and Ice Club, this pair produced many fine climbs in the Peak District. Limestone, for so long neglected because of its loose rock, was at last to come into its own. At first the emphasis was on artificial climbs, that is ones where the climbers use pitons driven into cracks in the rock for assistance. Soon, however, climbs were going 'free' and some magnificent routes were produced.

The modern era has seen many of the early artificial climbs done with fewer and fewer pitons, until apparently impossibly steep, and even overhanging, faces went without aid. Double ropes, increasingly sophisticated techniques of belaying, special high-friction rubber boots and chalk to stop sweaty hands slipping from the tiny holds, have all played a part in raising standards. Training, which until recently meant sinking a few pints in the pub, is now accepted and many climbers are high standard athletes. However, despite all the modern equipment which makes climbing safer, rock climbing is about risk, and solo climbing, where a fall is almost inevitably fatal, has attracted many top standard climbers.

Climbers will be seen at weekends and on summer evenings on all the gritstone edges, Stanage, Froggatt and the Roaches being among the most popular, while limestone cliffs, such as those in the Wye Valley and at Stoney Middleton, also receive great attention.

SELECTED WALKS IN THE PEAK DISTRICT NATIONAL PARK

Introduction to the Route Descriptions

1. ACCESS (see page 188) All of the walks described in this book follow public rights-of-way, concessionary paths or are on access land. Please do not take short cuts that may annoy local people. Occasionally some of the access land which is grouse moor may be closed during the shooting season (see page 188).

2. ASCENT The amount of climbing has been calculated from the Outdoor Leisure or appropriate Pathfinder map and is only approximate.

3. CAR-PARKS Three-quarters of the walks start from a public car-park. The rest start from a lay-by or a wide part of a public road, but

Previous page Path leading down to Monsal Viaduct

FIGURE 1 Signs used on detailed route maps

24

please take care when parking so as not to inconvenience others. Field gateways in particular should not be obstructed.

4. INTERESTING FEATURES ON THE ROUTE
5. LENGTH

These are marked on the map and in the text by corresponding numbers, e.g. *(1)*, *(2)*, showing where they can best be seen. Distances are in 'map miles', calculated from the relevant OS maps, with no account taken of ascent or descent.

6. MAPS

These are drawn to a scale of 1:25 000 using the symbols shown in fig. 1. Certain features have been exaggerated and others simplified to make them easier to read. Apart from Lyme Park and the north-eastern edges, all the walks are covered by either the Dark Peak or White Peak maps in the Outdoor Leisure series. Lyme Park is on Pathfinder sheet SJ 88/98 and the north-eastern edges are on sheet SK 28/38. (The whole area is also covered by the Peak District Tourist Map.) The names used are those appearing on these OS maps. The arrow on the maps is grid north and the appropriate sheets of the OS Landranger and Outdoor Leisure maps are shown on each map. In most cases the maps have been drawn so that the route goes from the bottom to the top of each page.

7. ROUTE DESCRIPTION

The following abbreviations are used:

L and R: left and right. Where these are used for changes of direction then they imply a turn of about 90° when facing in the direction of the walk. 'Half L' and 'half R' indicate a half-turn, i.e. approximately 45°.

PFS: Public Footpath Sign
PBS: Public Bridleway Sign
PWS: Pennine Way Sign
OS: Ordnance Survey

To avoid constant repetition, it should be assumed that all stiles and gates mentioned in the route description are to be crossed (unless there is a specific statement otherwise).

8. STANDARD OF THE ROUTES

The routes in this book cover a wide range of difficulty; from those which are within the capabilities of the youngest and oldest, to those which are only for tough and experienced walkers. However, it should be remembered that much of the land in the Peak District National Park is at an altitude of over 1000 ft (305 m), and on the high moors up to 2000 ft (610 m), and thus in bad weather the conditions can deteriorate very rapidly. While the weather in the surrounding low-lying areas can be quite pleasant, on the moors it can be misty, raining, or snowing, and a stiff valley breeze can becoming a raging gale higher up. What is in summer an easy stroll over, say, Bleaklow can turn in winter into a fight for survival. In winter also the roads in the Peak District frequently become blocked with snowdrifts; there are signs giving the road conditions over the passes, but it is still easy to become marooned.

The routes have been graded from easiest to hardest, taking into account the distance and height climbed as well as the difficulty of the terrain, as follows.

Easy (1) Walks of less than 6 miles (10 km), with no more than 1000 ft (300 m) of ascent, and which mostly stay on paths. The paths may go near cliffs or steep drops so that care is needed, and if the weather should deteriorate, paths that cross high open moors can be rather exposed.

Moderate (2) Longer walks up to 10 miles (16 km), some climbing to around 2000 ft (610 m) on exposed moorland where there is not always a clearly defined path, so care and compass work is necessary in bad weather.

More strenuous (3) From 10 miles (16 km) in length, some with rough walking over moorland. Route-finding ability is required, especially in bad weather.

Very strenuous (4) Long, rough and tough moorland walking, only suitable for the very experienced hill-goer.

Each walk commences with a description of the area, and details of the distance covered and height climbed, together with any special difficulties which may be met.

9. WEATHER FORECAST Local weather forecasts can be obtained from British Telecom's Weatherline.

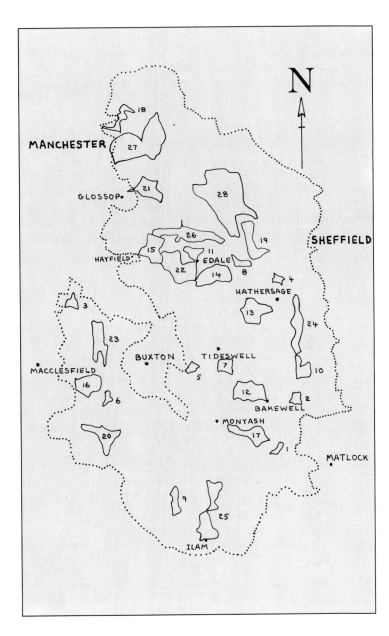

Opposite *Edale – the start of the Pennine Way*

FIGURE 2 The Peak District National Park. The routes described have been marked on and numbered.

10. STARTING AND FINISHING POINTS

All the walks are circular. The number of the appropriate Landranger (1:50 000) map with a six figure grid reference (see page 189) is given for the location of the starting and finishing point of each walk. A sketch map (fig. 2) shows the location of each walk within the Park.

11. TIME FOR COMPLETION

To estimate the length of time needed to complete a walk, fit walkers may use Naithsmith's formula, which is 3 miles (5 km) per hour plus one hour for every 2000 ft (610 m) of ascent. However, this does not allow for rests, food stops, photography, bad weather or difficulty of terrain, and most people will find that they have to allow more time than this for the walks.

1·1

Stanton Moor

STARTING AND FINISHING
POINT
Birchover. Cars may be parked with
care in the village (119-238622).
LENGTH
3 miles (5 km)
ASCENT
300 ft (90 m)

This small, attractive, heathery moor is covered with the evidence of past civilizations, including many stone circles and burial mounds. There are several interesting rocks, boulders and quarries to be seen, but please take care near the quarry edges.

ROUTE DESCRIPTION (Map 1)

Walk up the main street to a gate on the R (marked 'Barn Farm') at the end of the houses, opposite Ann Twyfords quarry *(1)*. Go up the farm road and to the R of the farm to a stile. Keep to the L of the fence to the gate and in the far corner of the next field a stile leads to a fenced path. At the end of the path turn half R over the stile, through the wall ahead at a gap and up to join the road at a stile in the hedge. Go L on the road for a few yards and turn R by the National Trust sign.

A fence follows the edge of Stanton Moor *(2)* for ½ mile

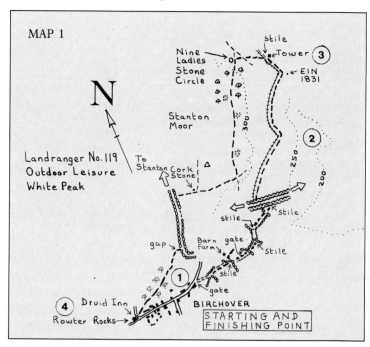

Opposite Stanton Moor

The tower on Stanton Moor

(800 m) before turning L at the large inscribed boulder (EIN 1831) in which footholds have been cut. After 150 yards (135 m), cross the fence at a stile behind the tower *(3)*. Go half R on the path which, in 200 yards (180 m), reaches Nine Ladies Stone Circle among the trees. Turn L and cross the open moorland for ½ mile (800 m) on a clear path. Turn R at the junction. Passing the Cork Stone, which can be ascended by means of metal rungs, the road is reached in ¼ mile (400 m). Turn L and just before the road turns L, go through a gap on the R and descend through the woods to the Druid Inn with Rowter Rocks *(4)* behind. Turn L back into Birchover.

1 Ann Twyfords Quarry

This is one of the few quarries still producing traditional millstones. They also manufacture grindstones which are used in engineering works, in glass bevelling and for knife sharpening. Large stones from the quarry are used in the manufacture of paper in crushing the wood to pulp and of course a lot of building stone is also produced.

2 Stanton Moor

On the eastern edge of the Peak District limestone, this outcrop of sandstone holds in its 150 acres (60 hectares) of heather-clad moorland one of the finest collections of Bronze Age remains to be found in the British Isles. Over seventy barrows are scattered across the moor, with examples of stone circles, cairns and standing stones; the best preserved is the Nine Ladies Stone Circle, 33 ft (10 m) in diameter, with its King Stone close by. This was once enclosed by a stone wall which has now been removed. A private museum at Birchover was established by J. and J.P. Heathcote, who from 1927 to 1950 excavated seventy cairns on the moor. Twenty-seven acres (11 hectares) of the moor were gifted to the National Trust in 1934.

3 Tower

At one time an inscription over the door read 'Earl Grey 1834' in tribute to the gentleman who carried the Reform Bill through parliament.

4 Rowter Rocks

This fascinating maze of caves, stairs and tunnels in the rocks is a delight to explore. Once thought to have connections with Druid culture, it was in fact the work of the local vicar, Thomas Eyre (died 1717), who built a study among the rocks and carved rooms, armchairs and alcoves. A rocking stone here was unseated by vandals – not recently however; it was the work of a group of fourteen young men on Whit Sunday in 1799.

EDENSOR AND CHATSWORTH PARK

STARTING AND FINISHING POINT
Calton Lees car-park just off B6012, Beeley–Baslow road (119-259684).
LENGTH
4 miles (6.5 km)
ASCENT
400 ft (120 m)

Although this walk follows public rights-of-way, a large part of the Chatsworth Estate is in fact freely open to the public to wander at will by the courtesy of the Duke and Duchess of Devonshire. Edensor village is a most charming place, while a visit to Chatsworth itself would complete a very pleasant day out.

ROUTE DESCRIPTION (Map 2)

From the car-park beside the B6012 walk towards the garden centre, through a gate ('No Thro' Road'), and follow the road

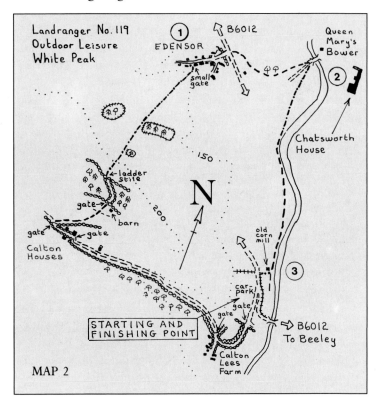

MAP 2

round the bend to the track junction by Calton Lees Farm. Go straight across through the gate and follow the track for ¾ mile (1·2 km) to Calton Houses. The track goes through a gate, between buildings, and out into the field at a gate. Turn R and the path leads across the field and into the wood at a gate to the L of a barn. To the R is Russian Cottage, named from the friendship between the sixth Duke of Devonshire and the Czar.

Emerging over a ladder stile into Chatsworth Park, aim just L of the spire of Edensor Church and cross the parkland. Enter Edensor *(1)* at a small gate and some steps by the church, and turn R past the fine stone cottages. Cross the B6012 to the gravel path opposite which climbs through a stand of beech trees with a good view of Chatsworth *(2)* ahead. Descend to the bridge and turn R to follow the river for a mile (1·6 km) to the old corn mill *(3)*. Climb up the bank and cross the road to the car-park.

1 Edensor

Pronounced 'Ensor', the present village is of very recent origin. In 1755 the views from Chatsworth were improved by the demolition of all that could be seen of the old village. In 1839 the rest of the village, although hidden in the valley bottom, was also demolished with the single exception of a cottage which still stands today isolated on the other side of the road. The new village was designed by Sir Joseph Paxton (of Crystal Palace fame), and the church of St Peter, consecrated in 1866, was the work of Sir Gilbert Scott. The past Dukes of Devonshire and their families lie in a quiet corner of the churchyard, but visitors come here to visit another grave, that of Kathleen Kennedy, daughter of Joseph Kennedy, United States Ambassador to Britain and sister of the late John Kennedy, President of the United States, whose visit on 29 June 1963 is commemorated on a plaque in front of the grave.

2 Chatsworth

This magnificent mansion is principally the creation of the first Duke of Devonshire who between 1686 and 1707 practically rebuilt the original house piecemeal and also built the great cascade in the grounds.

The first house on this site was built in 1552 by Sir William Cavendish and his celebrated wife, Bess of Hardwick. The house faced east and the Cavendish Hunting Tower, which dates from this time, remains in its splendid position on the hillside above the house. Queen Mary's Bower, a kind of

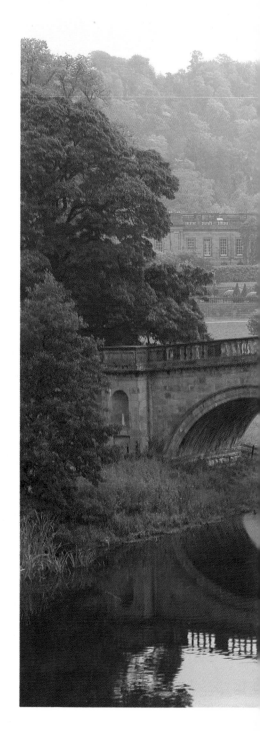

Chatsworth House

Edensor churchyard

summer house near the bridge and dating from the same time, encloses an ancient earthwork and was frequented by Mary Queen of Scots when she was a prisoner at Chatsworth in the custody of the Earl of Shrewsbury, Bess of Hardwick's fourth husband. Mary was here on five occasions between 1570 and 1581.

In the time of the fourth Duke the grounds were extensively remodelled under the direction of Capability Brown, and new roads, which ran north–south, replaced the former east–west alignment. The sixth Duke added the famous Emperor Fountain which throws a jet of water 290 ft (90 m) into the air, which when built was the second highest fountain in the world.

The house itself contains a splendid collection of treasures, paintings, tapestries, sculptures and other works of art, and in the grounds there are large herds of fallow deer.

3 *Old Corn Mill*

This mill, built about 1760 in a style complementary to Chatsworth House, was in operation, grinding corn, until 1950. A millstone still leans against an outer wall. During a gale in 1962 the building was badly damaged when trees fell on it, and now only the shell remains by the side of the River Derwent.

1·3

LYME PARK

STARTING AND FINISHING POINT
Lyme Hall car-park off the A6
Stockport to New Mills road
(109-963823).
LENGTH
4 miles (6.5 km)
ASCENT
550 ft (170 m)

Red deer roam freely across the moorland of Lyme Park, which
is now a Country Park providing pleasant walking with good
views across the Cheshire plain and also towards the wilder
Dark Peak to the east. Lyme Hall is a National Trust property
and is open to the public.

ROUTE DESCRIPTION (Map 3)

From the car-park turn L and follow the tarmac road up the
rise. At the top, strike off L and climb to join the wall, which
runs above the road, and follow it to a stile at the highest point.
Rounding the rhododendron bushes, go along the broad ridge to

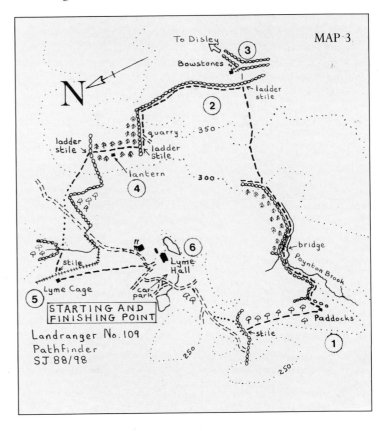

the ruin at Paddocks *(1)*. Turn L to the ruined wall which shortly joins a stouter wall and follow this, high above Poynton Brook in its steep-sided clough. In ¼ mile (400 m) a small stream is crossed at a bridge; then after another ¼ mile (400 m) turn R at the sign 'Bowstones' beside a gate into the wood. A climb of ½ mile (800 m) over the moor brings you to the edge of the park at Bowstonegate. Look out for red deer *(2)* near here.

To visit Bowstones *(3)*, which is situated by a house with a large collection of telecommunications aerials, cross over the ladder stile; but to continue the walk turn L inside the park wall. Reaching the highest point, the path starts to go downhill and then turns L with the wall to descend past a quarry on the L which once produced building stone. Leave the main path below the quarry staying by the wall to a ladder stile on the R. Cross Lantern Wood; about halfway through is the Lantern *(4)*. Emerging from the wood at a ladder stile, turn half L and aim directly for Lyme Cage *(5)* across the intervening valley. Cross the fence at a stile to reach the Cage, and then turn L along the ridge towards Lyme Hall *(6)*. On reaching the hall, turn R and follow the path back down to the car-park.

1 *Paddocks*
This ruined house dates from the seventeenth century and was used until 1936 to house employees of the Park. It consists merely of two rooms, one above the other, and has no water supply of its own.

2 *Red Deer*
The red deer is the largest of British mammals, an adult stag being about 4 ft high (1.2 m) at the shoulder. This is the only herd left in the National Park and there are about 250 animals descended from the wild herds which once roamed Macclesfield Forest centuries ago. The stags shed their magnificent antlers every year, but it is unusual to find these on the ground as the deer eat them for the mineral content.

3 *Bowstones*
These are the shafts of crosses dating from Anglo-Saxon times and are supposed to mark the frontier of an ancient kingdom – the word 'lyme' means boundary. They stood beside an old ridgeway and the heads of the crosses can now be seen at Lyme Hall.

4 *The Lantern*
Originally this was part of the Elizabethan hall at Lyme and was rebuilt here in the woods as a folly.

Moorland near Bowstones

5 *Lyme Cage*

Although the name suggests it may have once been used as a prison, this building housed men servants from the hall until 1920. Originally built around 1520, the structure was altered to its present form in the eighteenth century. Each face of the tower, except the north, carries a sundial.

6 *Lyme Hall*

This magnificent hall, presented to the National Trust in 1946, was the home of the Legh family for 650 years. The stone is local, having been obtained from quarries on the estate. The earliest building here was a hunting lodge, built in the fourteenth century by the first of the Legh family. The present building, the grandest house in Cheshire, is set amid 1300 acres (530 hectares) of parkland and dates in its present form from 1720 when the Italian architect Giacomo redesigned the preceding Elizabethan house. A few Tudor and Jacobean rooms remain from this earlier time.

Lyme Park near Poynton Brook

STANAGE EDGE

STARTING AND FINISHING POINT
Car-park by Dennis Knoll beneath Stanage Edge, north of Hathersage (110-227843).
LENGTH
4½ miles (7 km) or 3 miles (5 km) variant
ASCENT
500 ft (150 m)

Stanage is the most popular gritstone climbing edge in the Peak District. Within easy reach of Sheffield, the rocks attract climbers every weekend and during the summer evenings. At one time millstones were quarried here and piles of them may still be seen below the edge stacked on end awaiting the collection that will never come.

The visit to the old guidepost of Stanedge Pole may be omitted thus shortening the walk to 3 miles (5 km).

ROUTE DESCRIPTION (Map 4)

Walk up the main track and when it bends R by a small plantation go over the stile on the L. Climb the slope towards High Neb to meet a path near a large boulder. Turn R for a few yards and then up to the boulder which has several large millstones *(1)* beside it. A small path through the bracken then

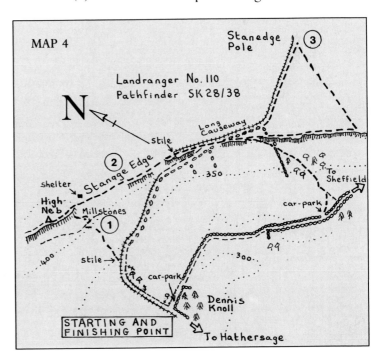

leads up to the rocks, passing more stacked millstones. At the foot of the rocks turn L and scramble up the heathery slopes to the path on the top of the rocks with the OS trig point of High Neb just to the L. Close by, there is a hollow in the rock identified by the number 9; about a hundred numbered basins like this can be found across the moor. These were carved at the beginning of the twentieth century by two gamekeepers to provide drinking water for the grouse. Hollow number 8 can be found on the jutting prow of rock nearby which is a good vantage point. On the top turn R. Walking back along Stanage Edge *(2)*, a useful shelter has been built a short distance off the path to the L. In ½ mile (800 m) a stile is crossed. When the main track comes in from the R, carry on along this to the boundary of open country.

The shorter variant now stays by the edge to join the return route which descends the edge by a paved trackway. The longer route goes half L keeping by the fence following the Long Causeway to Stanedge Pole *(3)*. Beyond the pole is Redmires Reservoir and to the L is Stanedge Lodge. Head now to the R back towards the edge; this path can be rather boggy in its middle section. At the edge turn R and in ½ mile (800 m), by a prominent boulder, the paved descent route is reached (also the shorter variant). This leads pleasantly downhill to Stanage Plantation passing the 'Grand Hotel', a gigantic fallen block with a bivouac cave beneath it. Beyond the wood fork R down to a car-park and into a lane. Turn R back to the start 1 mile (1·6 km) along the road.

1 Millstones

Piles of millstones lie beneath Stanage Edge; some of them flawed, but most of them stacked ready, then abandoned. From early Norman times gritstone has been used in corn milling, while Sheffield's cutlery and steel industry was founded on the proximity of the millstone grit which provided the grindstones.

The stones, which at Stanage were dug from the ground and in other places quarried, are of several different forms and sizes. The earliest ones are thinner, about 12 in (30 cm) deep at the centre tapering towards the outer edge, and 6–7 ft (1.8–2.1 m) in diameter. The Stanage stones are usually of a later type, from 3–7 ft (0.9–2.1 m) diameter, cylindrical and somewhat thicker. The stones were first cut to a hexagon and then trimmed to a circular shape while standing on a stone pedestal. They were next flattened on both sides and lastly

Looking west from Long Causeway on Stanage Edge

the central hole was made. As the stones would have been too heavy for transport by packhorses, sledges may have been used, or the stones may even have been rolled along. They were moved by waggons later.

The introduction of the superior French millstones in the mid-eighteenth century caused a dramatic fall in demand for the local product, which led the workers to riot, smashing the foreign stones in the mills. However by 1862, with the coming of the first roller mills, the end of the trade was in sight.

2 *Stanage Edge*

Probably the most popular climbers' crag in the Peak District, Stanage Edge is nearly 3 miles (5 km) in length with over 500 routes of all standards of difficulty. The earliest explorer of the delights of Stanage climbing was J.W. Puttrell who paid his first visit in 1890, pioneering several gully routes which are still climbed today. The greatest single advance in standards at Stanage was achieved in the 1950s by the legendary Joe Brown and the late Don Whillans; but standards never stay still and new and harder routes are still being produced on what may only be an outcrop, but which to its many devotees is as fine as many a mountain anywhere.

3 *Stanedge Pole*

Erected at a height of 1453 ft (443 m) on the Hallam moors, this was a landmark for jaggers leading packhorse trains. The pole, now encircled by protective iron bands, directed them on the route from Sheffield to Stanage Edge by way of the Long Causeway. A beautifully paved track which passes over the edge at the easiest point and slopes gently downhill to the plantation beyond is more recent and was probably built for the carriage of millstones. The pole is known to have been there in 1550, as this date is carved on the rock at its foot. Parish road surveyors who renewed it every fifty years have also carved their names on the rock.

1·5

CHEE DALE

STARTING AND FINISHING
POINT
Car-park on A6, Buxton–Bakewell
road. Opposite Topley Pike Quarry
(119-104725).
LENGTH
4½ miles (7 km)
ASCENT
500 ft (150 m)

Kingfishers and dippers skim the waters of the River Wye, which is crossed and recrossed many times by the huge arches of the disused Midland railway as it follows this narrow limestone valley. The old railway track is followed for a short way past the impressive cliffs of Plum Buttress, before descending to the river. At two places the path follows stepping stones in the river and after heavy rain these may become impassable, and you will have to retrace your steps. Therefore this walk is best kept for dryish conditions.

ROUTE DESCRIPTION (Map 5)

Follow the track beside the river away from the A6 and under two of the railway arches. In ½ mile (800 m), just before a third arch, turn R up some steps to join the disused railway (PFS 'Monsal Trail') *(1)*. Turn R on the railway past Plum Buttress *(2)* which towers above on the R. At the next bridge over the river turn L down a little path to the river (sign 'Chee Dale'). Cross the footbridge and turn R down steps to the river-bank. Soon

The River Wye, Chee Dale

the cliffs close in, overhanging the river, and you take to the stepping stones. In ¼ mile (400 m) the river enters a gorge. Two footbridges allow the river to be crossed and recrossed by the Nature Reserve, bypassing the gorge. Again the cliffs close in and only the stepping stones allow further progress. The cliff beyond overhangs considerably, while opposite are the sheer cliffs of Chee Tor *(3)*, also popular with climbers. The foot of Flag Dale is reached, with two footbridges and a stile just before Wormhill Springs which gush forth from beside the path. The dale soon widens out and at an iron footbridge after ¼ mile (400 m), double back up the hillside.

The path, with a natural paving of bare limestone, climbs gradually up the hillside and then swings away from Chee Dale and up to a stile and walled track which leads to the road. Turn L beside the road for a few yards and then L (PFS 'Great Rocks') at a stile. Go through the farm to a very small gate in the wall,

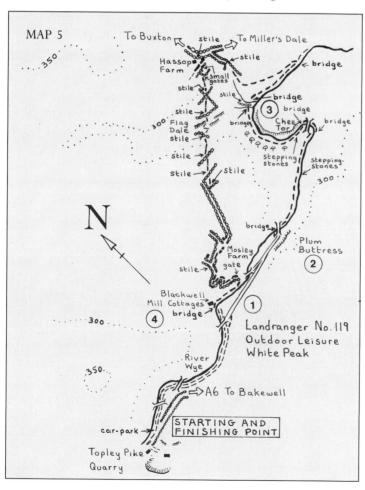

Chee Dale from the Wormhill road

half R to a similar gate and down to a stile in the corner. Continue in the same line to a stile above Flag Dale and zig-zag down into the dale. Climb steeply out of the dale to a stile and go straight ahead across the field to an indistinct stile. The next stile is to the R of the overhead lines and then, in the corner of the field beyond, a stile leads to a walled lane. Turn L down to the farm and R at the barn. Passing the farm, where the farm track turns R, turn L at a stile and zig-zag down the hill to a gate and under the railway. Turn R and walk beside the river to Blackwell Mill Cottages *(4)* to cross the river at a footbridge. The car-park is just over ½ mile (800 m) back up the track.

1 The Monsal Trail

The Peak Park Board negotiated with British Rail for twelve years before an agreement was reached which allowed the track to be put to new use in 1981 as the Monsal Trail. BR provided £154 000 towards the cost of repairs and although money is not yet available to improve the track surface in Chee Dale, making it rather rough walking on the old gravel ballast, it is a very attractive walk with spectacular views of the magnificent limestone cliffs.

The Buxton to Matlock railway, which reached Manchester in 1867, closed in 1968. The Great Rocks Dale to Doveholes section, however, is still in use, running through one of Europe's biggest quarries, principally for the supply of lime to the ICI works.

2 Plum Buttress

This is one of the finest limestone cliffs in the Peak District with several high standard climbs around 200 ft (60 m) in length, which ascend to the obvious horizontal slot, where the tiny figures of climbers will often be seen belayed. The routes then go over or around the overhanging face above.

3 Chee Tor

Another of Chee Dale's imposing limestone cliffs, whose most celebrated route is the Chee Tor Girdle. This, as its name indicates, traverses the cliff along the fault line, rather than, as is more usual with rock climbs, going straight up. This gives a rock climb of nearly 600 ft (180 m) in length, all of it exposed. The surrounding area is a Derbyshire Naturalist's Trust Nature Reserve.

4 Blackwell Mill Cottages

Surrounded by railway lines, these were built for railway workers and were serviced by a tiny railway station, Blackwell Halt, comprising one up and one down platform, each just long enough to take one carriage. The weir supplied Blackwell Mill, which has almost completely disappeared.

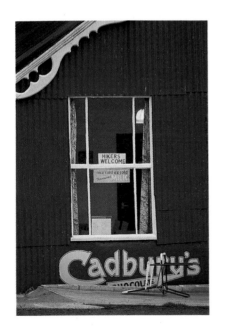

Café near Chee Dale

1·6

THREE SHIRE HEADS

STARTING AND FINISHING
POINT
Lay-by on A54 Congleton–Buxton
road near Danebower Quarries
(119-008699).
LENGTH
4½ miles (7 km) or 3 miles (5 km)
variant
ASCENT
700 ft (215 m)

The gritstone packhorse bridge at Three Shire Heads, where the counties of Derbyshire, Cheshire and Staffordshire meet, is not far from the road, but in a short walk you can feel very far away from the rush of the present day as you look down on Panniers Pool and think of the packhorse trains moving slowly through this countryside. In fact you are in the middle of a once industrial area which only recently has reverted to the wild state seen today.

The walk crosses the infant River Dane which in exceptionally wet weather can be difficult; if so, go out and back to Three Shire Heads by the return route.

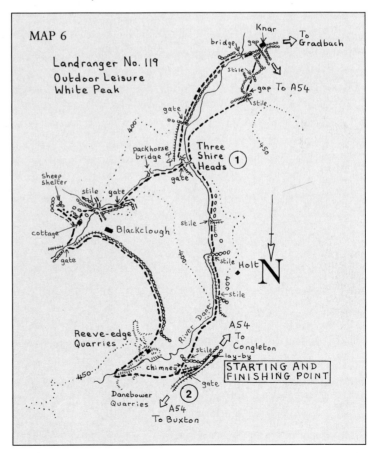

47

ROUTE DESCRIPTION (Map 6)

A few yards from the lay-by, towards Buxton, take the track towards a chimney which is all that remains of the Dane Colliery. Go through a gate and follow the track through Danebower Quarries to the River Dane. Cross the river, turn R and follow the track up to Reeve-edge Quarries and continue beside the wall.

The view gradually opens out as the track veers L away from the River Dane. The moorland on the R, pitted with depressions, speaks of the industrial past of this area when coal was dug from many small mines. Shortly you come to Blackclough Farm on the R and then the path rounds the head of a clough, crossing an iron gate.

As the main track bends L immediately above a small cottage, leave it and take a descending minor track which leads in roughly the same direction. Just before an unusual T-shaped sheep shelter, the right-of-way doubles back. Aim for the cottage, turn L through the gateposts, and head directly downhill to pass through a tumbledown wall. At the field corner the path meets the road by the entrance to Blackclough Farm. Turn R and take the R fork following the stream. Go through an iron gate and very shortly take the L fork continuing to follow the stream downhill, passing an interesting small packhorse bridge on the L, to reach Three Shire Heads *(1)* at a gate. The shorter variant now turns R over the bridge.

For the longer route do not cross the packhorse bridge ahead, but turn L and take the broad, sandy track which leads across another small bridge. Panniers Pool is the pool immediately below the bridges. In about 200 yards (180 m) pass through an iron gate and take the R fork along the wall. Follow the river until you come to a stout wooden bridge. Cross the bridge and climb up a steep track until Knar Farm is reached at a gate. Do not go through the gate, but turn immediately R onto a grassy track across the field. Go between gateposts at the next wall and then bear L up the hillside to a squeezer stile in the wall above. Turn R and follow the track rising gradually across the hillside through the next field and a small field beyond to emerge over a wooden stile onto a major track. Turn R and after a few yards a sandy track comes in from the L. This track leads gently downhill back to Three Shire Heads where the shorter route is rejoined.

Follow the River Dane upstream and at a five barred gate cross the stile on the R to stay by the river. Where the river

Reeve-edge Quarries

turns R, cross a stile and the field below Holt Farm. As the river meanders back, follow the fence until it meets the wall, where a stile allows you to rejoin the river-bank. A little further on, the ruins of a mine building herald the Dane Colliery (2) which would go unnoticed if it were not for the chimney. The track now leads uphill and over a stile, with the chimney straight ahead. Go through the gate above to rejoin the path back to the main road.

1 Three Shire Heads

At this charming spot by Panniers Pool, four packhorse ways meet to cross the River Dane. The bridge, if examined underneath, will be seen to have been widened on the upstream side, indicating the importance of the crossing and the heavy traffic it must once have seen. A map of 1610 calls this Three Shire Stones.

Packhorse trains, that is strings of up to forty or even fifty horses, were the principal means used for the transport of goods from the Middle Ages until the seventeenth century. Because packhorses could travel over the moors so much more easily than waggons, packhorses were being used in the Peak District well into the nineteenth century. Over boggy ground these tracks were paved with gritstone slabs which often can still be seen. It was, of course, much cheaper to maintain a narrow packhorse track than one for waggons, and bridges could be made narrower too. The name jagger, which occurs in some placenames such as Jaggers Clough on Kinder, was applied to the leader of a packhorse train and comes from Jaeger-galloway, the breed of horse most in use in the Peak District. The packhorses carried many varied loads, one of the earliest being salt, hence the name saltways.

The nearby village of Flash, which at 1518 ft (460 m) above sea level is claimed to be the highest village in England, depended on trade via the packhorse routes as the land hereabouts is poor. However, the ease with which one could escape the law by crossing into an adjacent county at Three Shire Heads led to a certain notoriety for Flash, and its name was applied to the coining of 'flash', or counterfeit, money by the inhabitants.

2 Dane Colliery

The coal mines in the Buxton area were never on the scale of those in the main industrial areas, but before rail transport brought in cheap coal from outside, these mines were important to the local community. Mining started at the beginning of the seventeenth century and continued until as late as World War I, although the principal activity occurred

Knar

in the period 1780 to 1880. The coal was used to burn limestone for use in mortar for building, and also in agriculture for improving the land.

The Blackclough Mine connected underground with the Dane Colliery. Dane Colliery produced some of the best and cleanest coal in the area; the coal of many other mines contained impurities such as sulphur and iron pyrites. The chimney, which is all that remains visible today, was connected by a flue running down the hillside to what was probably an engine house. The remains of the flue can still be seen in places. An opening near the river was the end of the sough or drainage level for the mine.

1·7

RAVENSDALE

STARTING AND FINISHING
POINT
Tideswell Dale car-park
(119-153743). 1 mile (1.6 km)
south of Tideswell.
LENGTH
5½ miles (9 km)
ASCENT
650 ft (200 m)

This walk should ideally be done in summer when Ravensdale (Cressbrook Dale) displays one of the greatest profusion and variety of flowers to be found anywhere in the Peak District.

The walk starts in Tideswell Dale where a basalt quarry has been reclaimed by the Peak Park Board who have removed the old machinery and grassed over the spoil heaps to provide an attractive picnic spot. Part of the dale has been declared a Site of Special Scientific Interest (SSSI). The walk continues along Miller's Dale (whose limestone cliffs are popular with rock climbers) down to Cressbrook Mill, and then Ravensdale is followed to the village of Litton.

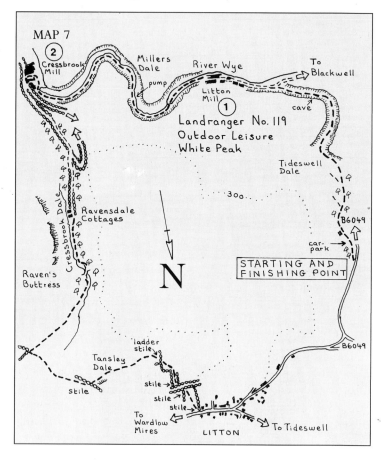

52

ROUTE DESCRIPTION (Map 7)

From the car-park take the track down Tideswell Dale. At the Y fork, branch R down the dale and at the next junction also fork R. Just before reaching the road, Tideswell Dale Cave is passed on the L close to the path. This is an old resurgence cave with a 100 ft (30 m) passage leading to a small chamber.

Join the road, turn L and follow the River Wye to reach Litton Mill *(1)* in about 200 yards (180 m). A concessionary path leads through the old factory and down beside the river. After a short while you will pass a small ruined waterwheel; this was once used to pump drinking water from a spring up to Cressbrook village above. Passing a swampy section of the river, the disused railway line to Bakewell and Derby may be seen where it emerges briefly from one of the tunnels at the top of a steep embankment beautifully constructed of limestone blocks. The river widens out to form a millpond, and at the end of this cross the leat by the bridge into the grounds of Cressbrook Mill *(2)*.

Emerging onto the road, turn L and immediately take the R fork, (sign 'Cressbrook and Litton'). Follow the road uphill under its canopy of trees and turn R (sign 'Ravensdale No Through Road') to the charming Ravensdale Cottages, built originally for mill workers. High above the trees on the opposite side of Ravensdale is Raven's Buttress whose limestone cliffs reach over 150 ft (45 m) in height. Take the narrow path straight ahead to the L of the cottage gardens.

Ravensdale is a 'dry' valley with a stream only during the wetter months. The path crosses a plank bridge and then forks. Take the clearer uphill path and, on reaching the valley rim,

Tideswell Dale

descend again to the L past grassed-over spoil tips of the old lead mines. Cross the wall at a wooden stile to follow Tansley Dale opposite (i.e. branching away from the main dale).

At the top of Tansley Dale a flight of steps leads up to a ladder stile. Cross this and head diagonally uphill to the wall corner ahead and to a stile onto a lane. Turn L and in a few yards clamber over the stile at the wall corner. Cross the field to the opposite corner, over the stone step stile onto the road, and turn L into Litton (meaning 'farm on a hill'), passing a cottage which dates from 1639. Hammerton Hall Farm is somewhat later in date, with 1768 picked out at the top of the rainwater down pipes. On the opposite side of the road, outside the Red Lion, are the village stocks, and close by is a gritstone cross. Take the road signposted 'Tideswell and Miller's Dale'.

At the T-junction onto the B6049, turn L onto this 1812 turnpike road. After ½ mile (800 m) a stand of fine mature beech trees on the L marks a footpath which leads back to the car-park.

1 *Litton Mill*

This mill, opened in 1782 for cotton spinning, was notorious for the exploitation of its workforce of apprentices imported from the London poorhouses. In an age when long hours and hard labour for children were common, Litton Mill's conditions, food and treatment were exceptionally bad, leading to the death of so many that burials were not conducted locally in order to avoid scandal. Most of the present buildings are late nineteenth century, and from 1934 until 1963 the mill produced silk and later man-made fibres.

2 *Cressbrook Mill*

The first mill, built around 1783, was destroyed by fire only two years later, but was promptly rebuilt and used for cotton weaving. The present building, now looking sadly dilapidated, dates from 1815 and was in use as a cotton mill until 1965. Although London apprentices were also employed here, the conditions were relatively better than at Litton Mill; the children worked six days a week and actually had a few hours off on a Sunday! Dale Terrace, the row of houses on the north side of the mill, was originally called Apprentices Row. The Gothic section at the end was probably a chapel.

The millpond dominates and fills the valley above the mill, and the footpath squeezes past it under overhanging lime-stone cliffs. There is a smaller millpond at the foot of Ravensdale on the opposite side of the road.

Woods at Tideswell Dale

WIN HILL FROM YORKSHIRE BRIDGE

STARTING AND FINISHING
POINT
Yorkshire Bridge off A6013, south of
Ladybower Reservoir (110-198850).
LENGTH
5 miles (8 km)
ASCENT
1000 ft (300 m)

Like its twin summit of Lose Hill across the Hope Valley, Win Hill is at the end of a ridge. Kinder throws down a long narrow spur towards the Ladybower Reservoir and the last outpost before the plunge into the valley is this splendid rocky summit. The initial ascent is very steep, but it is on a good path and once over the rest of the walk is nearly all downhill. The trees beside Ladybower Reservoir look particularly attractive in their autumn colours as the woods, although mainly conifers, are fringed with varied deciduous plantings.

ROUTE DESCRIPTION (Map 8)

From the bridge walk up towards Ladybower Reservoir *(1)* for a few yards and over the stile beside the gate. Turn L up the steps and cross the track of the old railway line *(2)* built during the construction of the Howden and Derwent Reservoirs. A stile marks the start of the ascent through the woods beside the stream, which for ¼ mile (400 m) is very steep indeed. When a track crosses the path, the angle eases and shortly a stile is crossed at a walled track. Go through the gap opposite and carry on uphill. Soon the trees are left behind and the open heather-clad moorland is reached. A ladder stile is crossed and the summit rocks of Win Hill *(3)* are only a short climb ahead.

Take in the view from the summit of Win Hill. To the north are the twin fingers of the Ladybower Reservoir, the Woodlands Valley, which runs west, and the Derwent Valley, which runs north up into the hills. From the fine rocky summit the path sets off westwards over the moorland following the broad ridge to meet and follow a wall for a short distance. To the L the Great Ridge, culminating in Lose Hill, is seen end on. The path then turns north-west, still following the ridge, until a wall is reached. Turn R on the far side and in a few yards enter the forest at a gap in the wall. Follow the forest track as it bends L and then R down to a major junction. Go straight across on the

now minor grassy track and then L to descend to meet the Ladybower Reservoir.

Woods above Ladybower

Turn R on the track which follows the attractively wooded shores of the reservoir for about 2 miles (3 km), finally passing the dam. The road then leads downhill back to the stile by Yorkshire Bridge. This bridge into Yorkshire was first recorded in 1599.

1 *Ladybower Reservoir*
Early plans were for several small reservoirs at the junction of the Ashop and Derwent Valleys; but this large one was eventually begun in 1935 and drowned the village of Derwent under the vast expanse of 6300 million gallons of water behind the massive dam at Bamford. Unlike the other two dams in the valley, Ladybower Dam is constructed with an earth embankment and clay core. Water is prevented from undermining the dam by concrete filled boreholes and a deep trench beneath the base of the dam. Ladybower Reservoir was completed in 1943 despite wartime difficulties with materials. It was opened by King George VI in September 1945 and took two years to fill. The dam is 1250 ft (380 m) long and 140 ft (45 m) high. At its base it is 665 ft (200 m)

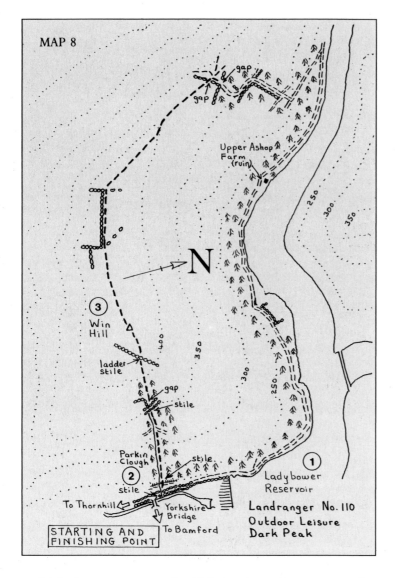

Map labels: MAP 8; gap; gap; Upper Ashop Farm (ruin); 250; 300; 350; N; ③ Win Hill; ladder stile; 400; 350; 300; 250; gap; stile; Parkin Clough; stile; ② stile; ① Ladybower Reservoir; To Thornhill; Yorkshire Bridge; To Bamford; Landranger No. 110 Outdoor Leisure Dark Peak; STARTING AND FINISHING POINT

thick, but tapers to only 17 ft (5 m) at the top (see also Derwent Village page 121).

2 *Old Railway*

See Derwent and Howden Reservoirs (page 185).

3 *Win Hill*

The summit at 1516 ft (462 m) was, according to legend, the camp of King Edwin of Northumbria who fought a bloody battle in the Hope Valley below against Cuicholm, the King of Wessex. The hill where King Cuicholm had made his camp became known as Lose Hill and the victorious King Edwin's campsite was known as Win Hill. It is more likely that 'win' refers to bilberries, while 'lose' is an old name for pigs.

The summit of Win Hill

58

1·9

THE MANIFOLD VALLEY

STARTING AND FINISHING
POINT
Car-park at Wetton Mill near
Butterton (119-095561).
LENGTH
5½ miles (9 km)
ASCENT
900 ft (280 m)

The Manifold Valley has, like its more famous sister Dovedale, limestone caverns and cliffs. However, as well as being usually much quieter it also has a disappearing river, Thor's Cave, which is in fact bigger than any in Dovedale and a veritable honeycomb of disused shafts and levels in the copper mines of Ecton Hill.

ROUTE DESCRIPTION (Map 9)

From the car-park, go over the bridge and L up the road to Dale Farm. Go through the farmyard to the L of the farmhouse, under the pipes ('Headroom 5 ft 8 in') and through the gate to walk up the dale. Continue until you come immediately below the Sugarloaf, a steep, limestone reef knoll, and skirt it to the L on a small path which climbs to a PFS. Go over the stile and then the one immediately to its L. Follow the fence and then the wall and, after crossing one more stile, reach a farm road ½ mile (800 m) beyond the Sugarloaf. Turn immediately L through the gate and, heading for Summerhill Farm, follow the R wall up to the next gate. Cross the field diagonally, passing an old lime kiln on the L, and go through a passage between walls into the next field. Cross this, again diagonally, to a similar passage, and turn half L to follow the wall through a gap and over a stile to turn R on a clear path a few yards down the hillside. In the valley below is Swainsley Hall, built in 1867 by a London solicitor, with a dovecote in its grounds. The Manifold Railway ran through a tunnel behind the hall, to conceal it from the owners.

The path stays level and then sweeps round the great bowl-shaped hillside above the Ecton Copper Mines (1), gradually dropping to the spoil heaps of the Dutchman Mine. Ahead is the engine house of Deep Ecton Mine and here the path doubles back along the ridge beside the wall, passing fenced, open mineshafts to a stile. The path continues on the L-hand side of the ridge, passing more shafts and levels, through two wall gaps and over three stiles to the ruined buildings of Waterbank Mine. From the mine, the road is reached after 300 yards (270 m) at a

Wetton Mill on the River Manifold

gate. Turn L down the road and, ignoring the L turning, continue through the gate and down the road for ½ mile (800 m) to Pepper Inn, now a private house, but once used as an isolation hospital when there was an outbreak of smallpox among navvies building the Manifold Light Railway.

A stile opposite leads to a small bridge over the stream, and then a wall on the R is followed up to a stile in the corner over the fence. Cross the field half L to the next stile and straight ahead over the brow of the hill to a stile with a quarry on the R. Crossing the stile ahead, go through the gate opposite and down the farm lane to the village of Wetton. Turn R and walk through the village to the far end. Turn R at the T-junction and then L at the fork (sign 'Concession Footpath'). In just under ½ mile (800 m) go through a gate and over the stile to the R (PFS). Go L down to the gap in the ruined wall at the corner, across the dip and up to a stile. A short steep climb leads to the summit of the cliffs above Thor's Cave. Be very careful; the cliff edge is unprotected and quite sheer.

Return the same way and turn L to circle down to the base of the cliffs at the entrance to Thor's Cave *(2)*. Once this huge natural cavern has been explored, a flight of stone steps will lead you down to the River Manifold. The river is usually dry, but is crossed by a substantial bridge. Turn R on the old track of the Manifold Light Railway *(3)* and in ½ mile (800 m), crossing another bridge, turn L to follow either of two parallel roads back to the car-park at Wetton Mill *(4)*.

1 Ecton Copper Mines

In the eighteenth century, Deep Ecton Mine was a very profitable mine for its owner the Duke of Devonshire, with

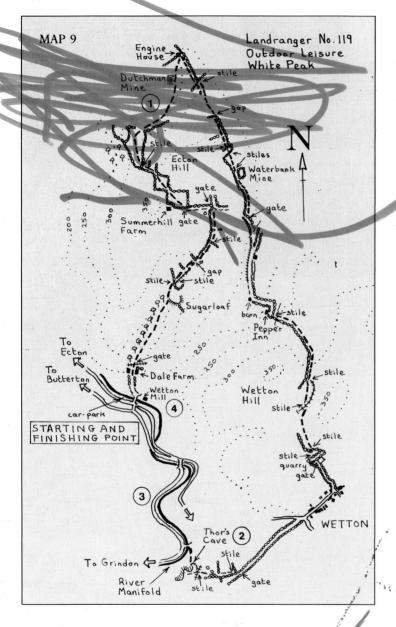

Map content:

MAP 9

Landranger No. 119
Outdoor Leisure
White Peak

Engine House
Dutchman Mine
stile
gap
(1)
stile
stile
stiles
Ecton Hill
Waterbank Mine
N
gate
gate
350
300
250
200
Summerhill gate
Farm
stile
stile
gap
stile
Sugarloaf
barn
stile
Pepper Inn
To Ecton
gate
250
stile
To Butterton
Dale Farm
300
350
stile
Wetton Mill
(4)
Wetton Hill
250
car-park
stile
350
STARTING AND FINISHING POINT
stile
quarry gate
(3)
WETTON
Thor's Cave
(2)
stile
To Grindon
stile
gate
River Manifold

profits amounting to over one million pounds. It was, at 1380 ft (420 m), the deepest mine in Great Britain.

Deep Ecton Mine was just one of a number of copper mines to be found at Ecton, all of which are now disused and in ruins. The Ecton copper mines also saw in 1670 the earliest use in Britain of gunpowder in mining and at its peak around 300 men, women and children worked here. Sixty men worked a six-hour shift for about 5p, while boys removed the ore to be crushed above ground by women and girls.

Near Alstonefield

Although the Ecton copper mines did not suffer the serious water problems often found elsewhere in the Peak, a 32 ft diameter (10 m) waterwheel was built underground to power drainage pumps and boats were used as transport some 200 ft (60 m) beneath the River Manifold. The engine house, still in use as a barn, held a Boulton and Watt engine which raised waste rock to the surface, forming great spoil heaps since removed for road making. The mines finally ceased production in the late nineteenth century.

2 *Thor's Cave*

Thor's Cave, the cave of the Norse Thunder God, looks down on the Manifold Valley from a very large main entrance, 30 ft (9 m) high and over 20 ft (6 m) wide. A second side entrance, West Window, faces down the valley. First excavated by Samuel Carrington from Wetton in 1864, the cave has yielded stone querns, pottery fragments, bronze brooches, iron knives and bones from Romano-British times. Much has probably been lost by the early excavators who made a large spoil heap outside the cave entrance. The pieces of tape seen hanging from high in the roof are left by rock climbers whose spectacular climb 'Thor' goes up the wall, crosses the roof and then ascends the cliff.

3 *Manifold Light Railway*

Opened in 1904 and closed again by 1934, this railway fell between the heyday of steam and the modern preservation societies who would surely have rescued it. It took two years to build and was said by a navvy to 'start from nowhere and end up in the same place'. A private, narrow gauge railway of 2 ft 6 in (762 mm), it operated mainly as a milk train, supplementing meagre passenger traffic with excursion trains at weekends and public holidays. There was a connecting milk train from the main line at Waterhouses from 1919 and 300 churns a day were carried. When the dairy closed in 1933 the railway rapidly succumbed, being converted to a footpath in 1937.

4 *Wetton Mill*

Wetton Mill, now a farm, but originally a corn mill, was first mentioned in records of 1577. The bridge is much later, dating from 1807. Just above the bridge at Wetton Mill is a limestone hummock, full of interesting holes, known as Nan Tor Cave. The River Manifold disappears just below the mill and travels 5 miles (8 km) underground before reappearing at the 'Boil Hole' in the grounds of Ilam Hall. Sir Thomas Wardle of Swainsley Hall unsuccessfully attempted to block the swallow holes with concrete, but the river won and only sometimes, usually in winter, appears above ground.

2·10

WELLINGTON'S AND NELSON'S MONUMENTS

STARTING AND FINISHING
POINT
Curbar Gap National Park car-park
east of Curbar (119-261748).
LENGTH
6½ miles (10.5 km)
ASCENT
850 ft (260 m)

This visit to the matching monuments to Nelson and Wellington, which face each other across the valley, contrasts the grandeur of the rugged and wild edges with the formality of Chatsworth Estate.

ROUTE DESCRIPTION (Maps 10, 11)

Turn R out of the car-park where there is a prominent guidestone which marked the junction of several old packhorse routes, and in a few yards turn L at a stile by the sign 'Boundary of Open Country'. Notice also the important admonition nailed to the tree 'No manure removal', so be sure to clean your boots! Either follow the wide track which leads to the Eagle Stone, or the edge of the escarpment where the view is better. Passing the Eagle Stone *(1)*, reach the edge and turn L to arrive at Wellington's Monument *(2)*.

Walk east from Wellington's Monument along the broad footpath on the edge of the moor, which is fringed with silver birch and rowan. Shortly before the main road there is another guidestone on the R which is inscribed 'CHESTE RFEILD ROADE' ('Road to Chesterfield'). Unusually it is marked on one face only. On reaching the road at a gate, turn R downhill to the crossroads. Crossing over the A621, take the ladder stile at the boundary to open country. Bear almost immediately L off the major track and follow the track heading directly for Birchen Edge. The ground to the left of this track is out of bounds. After scattered birch trees and some boggy ground, a short steep climb on a narrow path to the L leads to the top of the edge close to the OS trig point.

The crag reaches its highest point at Nelson's Monument *(3)*, a less imposing memorial than Wellington's and often treated with scant respect by climbers who use it as a belay. Follow the path along the edge and, at the Water Board manhole covers, the path turns R and descends the edge. Upon reaching the

Birchen Edge near Nelson's Monument

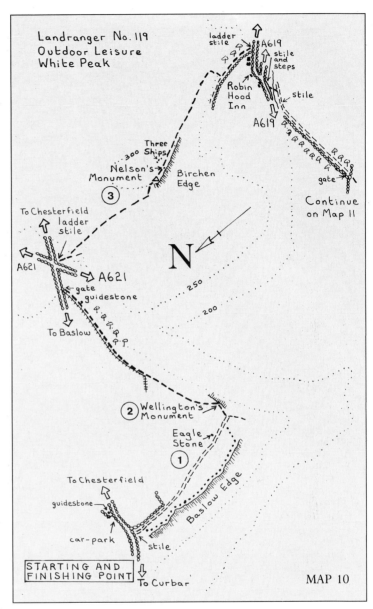

Curbar from Baslow Edge

broad path at its foot, turn L with a golf course on your R. At the main road climb a ladder stile over the wall and turn R down the road to join the A619 at the Robin Hood Inn.

Shortly after the Eric Byne campsite entrance, cross the A619 and take the path at the wooden sign 'Concessionary Footpath to Baslow'. A steep flight of steps leads down to a stout wooden bridge. Joining a broad track, turn R and follow the yellow waymarks of the concessionary footpath over a stile and along the lane for ½ mile (800 m) to a gate into a field. At the next

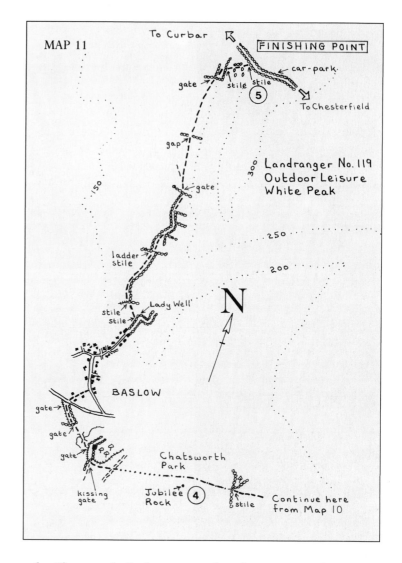

stile Chatsworth Park is entered and in 300 yards (270 m) Jubilee Rock *(4)* will be found a few paces off the track to the L. Follow the indistinct path across the open parkland, marked occasionally with yellow waymarks, to leave Chatsworth Park at 'The Kissing Gate'.

In 50 yards (45 m) turn L through a small kissing gate into the field and then across the hump-backed bridge. Cross the next field to a gate. Go along a path flanked by a stone wall and fence to a flight of steps which will bring you into Baslow at a gate just before the road. Cross the road and go up the narrow path opposite, just to the R of 'Ashton Fields' house. Turn L onto the next road. At Barr road turn R and, where the metalled surface deteriorates to a track just before Lady Well, turn L through a stile.

Follow a rising grassy path to a stile and through the fields to

Climbers on Curbar Edge

the L of a wall to a ladder stile. Joining a more major track, follow this between gritstone walls to emerge again onto open country at a gate below Baslow Edge. At the Y-fork take the R branch and continue at the same level on a sandy path through the bracken. At the open country sign, go through a gate onto a wide, green lane which rises to meet the road near Curbar Gap. Turn R at the National Trust sign and through a squeezer stile to avoid the road walking. Emerging onto the road at a stile, a gritstone slab on the R is inscribed with a Biblical text *(5)*. The car-park is a few yards up the road.

1 *Eagle Stone*

Many years ago the young men of Baslow were required to demonstrate their fitness for the responsibilities of marriage by ascending this rock. Nowadays it is the rocks of the edge itself which attract climbers, and anyway, as the climber Morley Wood once said of the climb 'Bachelor's Buttress' at the Roaches, 'Married men are more used to taking risks than bachelors'. These crags are sometimes used by the mountain rescue teams for practising lowering stretchers down the rockface. The quarry on the edge at this point was in use as late as the 1930s.

2 *Wellington's Monument*

The monument is inscribed 'Wellington Born 1769 Died 1852. Erected 1866 by E.M. Wrench late 34th Reg'mt'. From here there is a good view across the valley to Gardom's Edge and also to Nelson's Monument.

3 *Nelson's Monument*

This monument was erected in 1810 by John Brightman, a Baslow man, predating Wellington's Monument by some fifty years. The date 1865 inscribed on the obelisk appears to point to graffiti not being a modern phenomenon. There are three rocks nearby commemorating the ships of Nelson's fleet, *Victory*, *Defiant* and *Royal Soverin*.

4 *Jubilee Rock*

Chatsworth Park was the creation of the fourth Duke of Devonshire, 1720–1764, who employed the landscape architect Lancelot (Capability) Brown. The shape of the woods which follow the contour of the hills is typical of Brown's work. Situated in the park, the Jubilee Rock, carved to commemorate Queen Victoria's golden jubilee, reads:

1837

SEND HER	V	HAPPY
VICTORIOUS	I	AND GLORIOUS
	T Ⓒ R	
LONG TO	I	GOD
REIGN OVER US	A	SAVE THE QUEEN

1887

5 *Biblical Text*

This slab is inscribed 'Hebrews 7 25' and is one of several such slabs in the vicinity which were carved by Edwin Gregory, a mole-catcher and local preacher.

2·11

RINGING ROGER AND GRINDSLOW KNOLL

STARTING AND FINISHING POINT
Edale car-park (110-124853).
LENGTH
6 miles (9 km)
ASCENT
1200 ft (375 m)

This popular walk from Edale encircles the Grindsbrook Valley keeping close to the edge of the Kinder plateau. There is the feel of the mountains about this walk with the steep drop into the valley always at your side. After a strenuous ascent, Ringing Roger is reached, and, from the summit rocks round to Grindslow Knoll, walkers can be seen far below on their way up Grindsbrook Clough at the start of their long journey north on the Pennine Way.

ROUTE DESCRIPTION (Map 12)

From the car-park turn R under the railway bridge and up into Edale village (1) to the Old Nag's Head. Follow the signs for the Pennine Way (2) up the unsurfaced track to the iron gates. A

Nether Tor

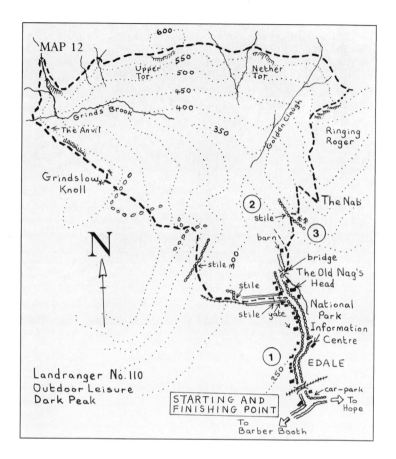

PWS points R on a path which leads down some steps to a bridge. Go along the footpath a short way to a small barn and then turn R and follow the clear path up the field to a stile by Fred Heardman's Plantation *(3)*. The path zig-zags up the hillside to The Nab, which is a good viewpoint for the Vale of Edale spread out below. Contour round towards Golden Clough until you reach the spot immediately below Ringing Roger, and then strike up the hillside directly to the rocks. From the summit, head towards an area of bare rock and sand, and then turn L onto the path which keeps to the edge of the plateau. Crossing Golden Clough, the rocks of Nether Tor on the L are where the stone for Edale Church was quarried.

The path continues along the edge passing the highest point at Upper Tor where Pym Chair can be seen on the distant skyline to the west. Continue to the head of Grindsbrook Clough where it is necessary to turn R and detour for 200 yards (180 m) to avoid the great ravine. Double back on the far side and follow the path round towards Grindslow Knoll, passing the Anvil Stone. The summit of Grindslow Knoll, in just over ¼

Golden Clough

mile (400 m), can be missed as the path does not cross the highest point which is a few yards off to the R.

Descend now south-east towards Edale far below. Soon the eroded path improves to a track which leads down to a stile and fields beyond. Cross the field towards a fence and then cross a wall at a stile. A sunken path between hedges is joined, which soon arrives at a stile and a kissing gate opposite the Old Nag's Head. Turn R and walk back down the road to the car-park.

1 Edale Village

The village of Edale, the island valley, has two pubs, both of which at one time came under the jurisdiction of Fred Heardman (see *(3)*). There is also a café, an excellent Peak Park Information Centre and several campsites. Despite Edale's popularity, it has not been spoilt and manages to retain much of its charm. Five packhorse ways converged here and there is a good example of a narrow packhorse bridge crossing Grinds Brook only yards from the Old Nag's Head.

2 The Pennine Way

Britain's first and most celebrated long-distance footpath stretches 250 miles (400 km) from Edale in the south to Kirk Yetholm over the border in Scotland. This high level route, which follows the Pennine backbone of England, was conceived by Tom Stephenson in 1935; but it took thirty years of dedicated and persistent negotiation before it was finally opened on 24 April 1965. As many as 10 000 people a year start on the route, and, although not all of these complete the walk (it is a tough undertaking), its popularity has led to erosion problems such as the four-lane highway up Grindsbrook Clough.

3 Fred Heardman's Plantation

This plantation is dedicated to the memory of Fred Heardman, a legendary figure of the Peak District who was, for many years, the landlord of both the Old Nag's Head and the Church Inn (now the Rambler Inn). Known to his friends as Bill the Bogtrotter for his exploits on arduous walks and runs in the Peak, he became a rural district councillor and fought, fortunately very successfully, against the industrialization of this attractive valley. He was also a member of the Peak District Branch of the Council for the Preservation of Rural England, and when the Peak District National Park was formed, the Nag's Head became their first information centre and mountain rescue post.

Ringing Roger

MONSAL DALE AND ASHFORD IN THE WATER

STARTING AND FINISHING POINT
White Lodge car-park (119-170705). On the A6 Buxton–Bakewell road, 3 miles (5 km) west of Bakewell.
LENGTH
8½ miles (13.5 km)
ASCENT
800 ft (240 m)

The lower reaches of the River Wye pass through Monsal Dale, spanned by the great viaduct of the old Buxton to Derby railway, and on down past the village of Ashford in the Water, which is famed for its well dressing, to the town of Bakewell.

Packhorse bridges and old mills blend into the scene, complementing the natural beauty of the dale; while the railway itself becomes in summer a wild flower garden which links with the Wye to form a varied and interesting walk.

ROUTE DESCRIPTION (Maps 13–15)

Cross the A6 to a stile in the wall opposite. Descend to a small stream and over a wooden ladder stile, where in summer the banks of the stream are covered in the bright yellow flowers of musk. Through the woodland beyond (PFS 'Monsal Dale') the first view of the River Wye is seen. On the opposite bank is Fin Cop, whose top is the site of an Iron Age hill fort.

Follow the river upstream for 1¼ miles (2 km) to a stile and under Monsal Viaduct *(1)*. At the footbridge over the river, turn half L through the stile (PFS 'Brushfield and Taddington Dale') and ascend to the disused railway. Go over the stile (sign 'Monsal Trail') to join the railway where the blocked up entrance of a lead mine can be seen opposite. Turn L towards the tunnel to emerge suddenly on the very exposed heights of Monsal Viaduct. Just before the tunnel turn L and after 100 yards (90 m) turn R onto another track. Continue to climb until a flight of stone steps brings you out, somewhat breathless, to Monsal Head (café, pub and toilets).

Cross the B6465 and take the road opposite (an old turnpike) to Little Longstone. Passing the Congregational Church, enter the village and go past (or through!) the Packhorse Inn to turn R over a stone step stile (PFS 'Ashford 1½ ml') just past the last house on the R. Bear half R across four fields to rejoin the tracks of the disused railway.

Opposite Sheepwash Bridge, Ashford in the Water

76

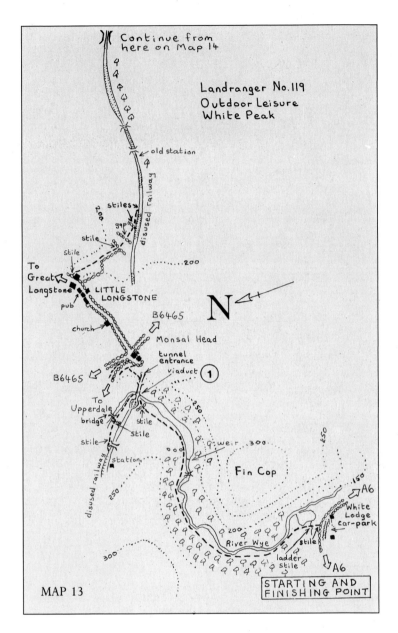

Continue from here on Map 14

Landranger No.119
Outdoor Leisure
White Peak

old station

disused railway

stiles

gap

stile

stile

To Great Longstone

LITTLE LONGSTONE

pub

church

B6465

200

N

B6465

Monsal Head

tunnel entrance

viaduct ①

To Upperdale bridge

stile

stile

stile

disused railway

station

weir 300

Fin Cop

250

150 A6

White Lodge car-park

200

River Wye

stile

300

ladder stile

A6

MAP 13

STARTING AND FINISHING POINT

Turn L on the railway and in ¼ mile (400 m) pass through the old station at Thornbridge Hall. Soon the view to the L opens out with Longstone Edge forming the skyline in the distance. One mile (1.6 km) beyond the station, opposite the Rowdale toll-bar house, with the bell and gate symbol on its gable, take the footpath turning R through a wooden gate (PFS 'Bakewell'). Follow the green path, enclosed by stone walls, over the hill through seven gates to a track to the road.

Go straight ahead to cross Holme Bridge (2) and then R onto the A6. Just after the factory, turn R through a stile. Cross the field and go through a narrow path between the houses crossing

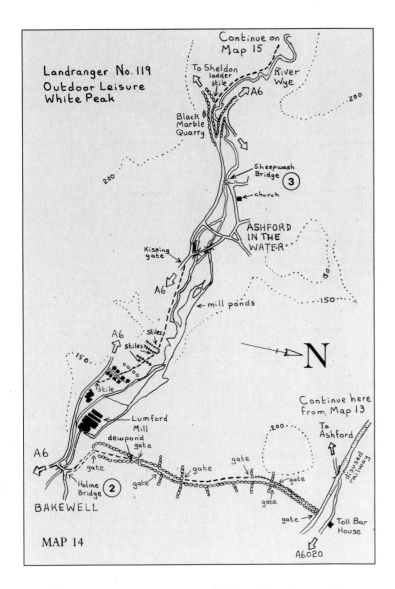

MAP 14

a road to emerge again into open fields. Follow the meadows to Ashford, over three stiles and passing the millponds, to emerge onto the A6 at a kissing gate. Turn R to cross the two bridges (the second dated 1664). Over the road, enter Ashford in the Water *(3)* and turn L by the village store to pass the Church of the Holy Trinity. At the end where the street turns R, Sheepwash Bridge will be seen on the L. Turn L over the bridge to the A6. Cross this and turn R to gain the relative safety of the footpath on the far side. After about 300 yards (260 m) take the minor road (PFS 'Monsal Dale avoiding A6 road'), passing on the L the Ashford Black Marble Quarry (worked until 1905). Two hundred yards (180 m) along this road, just past a recently restored bridge on the site of the Black Marble Mill, turn R (PFS 'Monsal Dale via White Lodge') and over a ladder stile.

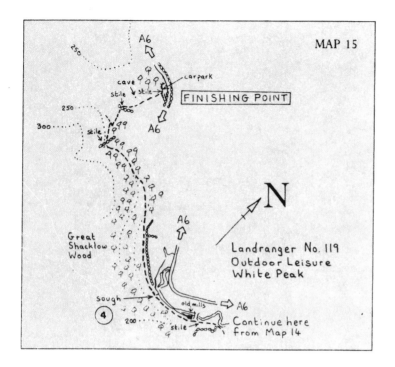

Follow the fields beside the river for ½ mile (800 m) to a stile and the remains of old mills, one of which used to pump drinking water up to Sheldon. Go behind the mills into Great Shacklow Wood and in 200 yards (180 m) the sough of Magpie Mine *(4)* will be seen entering the river on the R. The path now climbs up the hillside and in ⅔ mile (1.1 km) descends to a stile. Continue to the lowest point of the path and turn R (PBS 'Bridleway to A6'). Cross the stile, turn R, and shortly before arriving back at the car-park there is, hidden in the trees above, Taddington Dale Resurgence Cave from which a stream issues in wet weather.

1 Monsal Viaduct

Monsal Viaduct is a most spectacular feature. Built in 1867, the Midland railway ran here until it was closed in 1968, and now the viaduct has been declared of architectural and historic interest. John Ruskin, the nineteenth-century English author and art critic, was less enthusiastic about the railway, declaring 'You enterprised a railroad through the valley – you blasted its rocks away, heaped thousands of tons of shale into its lovely stream. The valley is gone and the Gods with it, and now every fool in Buxton can be at Bakewell in half an hour and every fool in Bakewell at Buxton; which you think a lucrative process of exchange – you Fools everywhere.'

Monsal Dale and the viaduct from Monsal Head

If the weather is unkind it is worth knowing that by turning R instead of L on joining the railway, one of the old buildings of the Monsal Dale railway station will be found still standing.

2 *Holme Bridge*

This was rebuilt in 1664 on a packhorse route to the north. The bridge was probably built at this point in order to avoid payment of tolls at Bakewell itself. A corn mill at Bakewell, recorded as far back as the *Domesday Book*, was supplied with water from this river. When, in 1778, Lumford Mill was built by Richard Arkwright and a reservoir was constructed for the new mill, a bypass leat was built to feed the old mill; this however was not entirely adequate for the purpose, to the annoyance of its owner the Duke of Rutland. In 1852, with the addition of two larger waterwheels to Lumford Mill, another reservoir was constructed upstream, as well as a new channel; while a weir was built in the river to improve the supply to the corn mill.

3 *Ashford in the Water*

Ashford in the Water is one of the villages which continues the ancient tradition of well dressing. About 150 years ago the present floral patterns were introduced. Petals, berries, bark and suchlike are pressed into a bed of clay to form beautiful pictures and patterns. As many as five wells are dressed in Ashford for Trinity Sunday and can be seen for the following week.

Sheepwash Bridge is a medieval packhorse bridge; 'sheepwash' refers to the practice of washing sheep by driving them into the river and making them swim across to emerge on the other side.

The name Ashford comes from the Saxon 'Aescforda', where the Old Portway forded the river, and is mentioned in the *Domesday Book* with a reference to 'plumbariae' or places where lead was smelted.

4 *Magpie Mine Sough*

The sough, or drainage tunnel, drains the Magpie Mine. The scree above the entrance indicates the site of the massive explosion which tore this hillside apart and partially blocked the river on 23 April 1966. Water had built up behind a blockage in the mine and eventually burst forth, fortunately without injuring anyone. The Magpie Mine was being worked for lead as early as 1795 and probably earlier than that. The Peak District Mines Historical Society use the main buildings at Sheldon as a Field Centre. The Magpie sough, driven in 1873, and large enough to be navigable by boat, was probably one of the last major soughs dug in this area.

2·13

ABNEY MOOR AND BRETTON CLOUGH

STARTING AND FINISHING POINT
Great Hucklow to Eyam road (119-190781).
LENGTH
8½ miles (13.5 km)
ASCENT
800 ft (240 m)

Abney Moor

Abney Moor, an isolated piece of moorland cut off from the larger and wilder northern moors by Hope Valley, is a quiet and peaceful place where the gliders from Great Hucklow soar in the sky above. The beauties of Bretton Clough will also be appreciated by connoisseurs of the Peak District, with its pleasant tree-lined streams in little steep-sided valleys.

Eyam Edge, the starting point, is an excellent viewpoint. Northwards is Stanage Edge, and through a gap in the intervening hills Win Hill and Derwent Edge can be seen.

ROUTE DESCRIPTION (Maps 16–18)

Cross the stile and descend the very steep field beside the wall. On the R is an interesting series of hummocks and hills which are the result of landslips. Bretton Brook ('Bretton' meaning 'farm of the Britons') at the foot of the slope is crossed by a footbridge and the track followed uphill to a stile on the L. Continue straight ahead, keeping near the wall, to the next stile on the R; and then head L of the farm to cross a stile onto the farm track. Turn L towards the road and then R to a stile (PFS 'Bradwell') which gives access to Abney Moor.

Follow the clear path across Abney Moor for 1 mile (1.6 km). On many days gliders from the Great Hucklow Gliding Club *(1)* circle high in the sky above the moor. Leave the moor over a stile onto the old packhorse way from Bradwell to Eyam. Turn R and follow it for about ¾ mile (1.2 km), past the end of the road down to Abney (PBS) until the wall turns R . Turn L (PBS), and in 100 yards (90 m) go through gateposts on to the walled Shatton Lane. Straight ahead, the Great Ridge of Mam Tor to Lose Hill can be seen across the valley. Follow the old lane for 1 mile (1.6 km) with Shatton Edge on the R, first through a gate and then past a tall TV repeater mast, until the lane turns L just after another gate. A ladder stile at the corner leads back to the moor and in a few yards a wall comes in from the L. Follow this wall

83

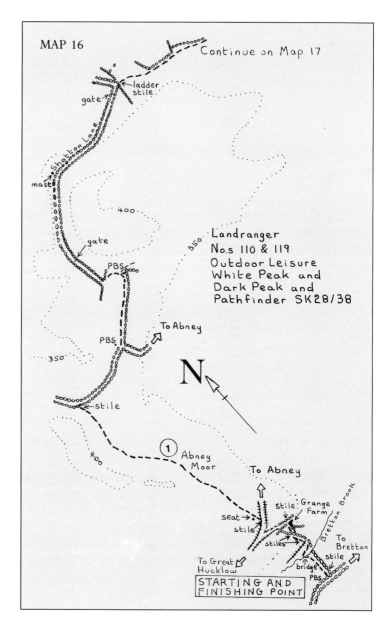

for about a mile (1.6 km) until the road is met near Offerton Hall at a stile. Turn R onto this and walk uphill. In ¼ mile (400 m) a stile on the L leads to an attractive footpath which is followed down to a stile just before Callow Farm. At the farm, turn L and through a small gate. Go downhill, crossing a broken wall, and enter the wood at another small gate below the farm.

Go through the wood and out into a field at a stile. Cross the field and turn R out of the gate onto the lane, which after about ¼ mile (400 m) passes the entrance to a house and leads up to the road. Go straight across the road, over a stile and half L up the field to another stile on the top of the ridge. Now go R and downhill where a line of signposts leads to the farm road. The bridge immediately below and the stile on its far side lead to a field whose L-hand wall should be followed up to a gate and lane. At the top of the lane turn R and go down towards Tor Farm, passing through a gate on the L just before the farm. Beside the wall a path leads through three field gateways and then a gate into woodland. After passing over a stile in the wood and a stream, the track climbs steadily up the hill through oak and silver birch onto the moorland. In ½ mile (800 m), and having crossed a small clough, Stoke Ford is reached, which is the meeting of several old tracks and has a bridge across the main stream.

Turn L at Stoke Ford (not across the bridge) and climb uphill. In a few yards the track forks. Take the R fork which follows Bretton Brook. In ¼ mile (400 m) you come to a stile and then a little, steep-sided clough. Climbing out of the clough past a ruined barn, go through four ruined walls and into woodland where on meeting a fence turn L to follow it down to a stile and stream. Zig-zag up the hillside and over a stile into fields. Follow the R-hand wall to another stile onto a farm lane. In ¼ mile (400 m) the lane comes out at the Barrel Inn. Turn R and ¾ mile (1.2 km) down the road is the starting point.

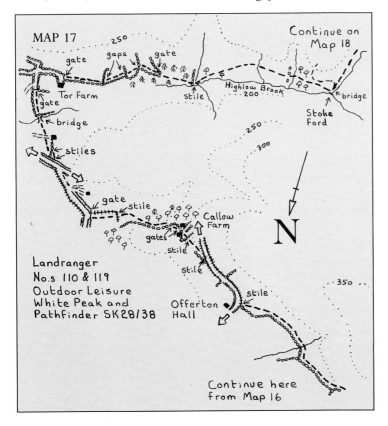

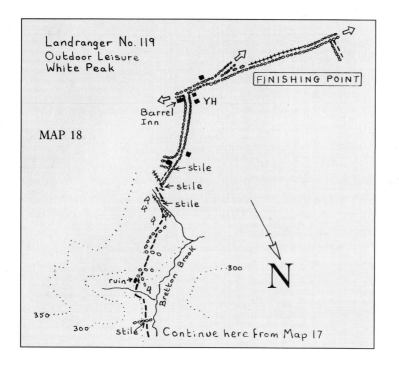

Landranger No. 119
Outdoor Leisure
White Peak

MAP 18

FINISHING POINT

YH

Barrel
Inn

←stile

←stile

←stile

ruin→

Bretton Brook

·300

350····

300

stile   Continue here from Map 17

N

1 Great Hucklow Gliding Club

The club, officially known as the Derbyshire and Lancashire Gliding Club, was formed in 1935 by a group of local flyers, who leased Camp Hill, and the Manchester Aeronautical Society, who flew from the Barrel Inn in 1934. The remains of an Ancient Briton fort on the south and south-west edge of Camp Hill also cut across the field to the inconvenience of the club. The field itself is private property.

There was a break in flying during World War II when the club was banned from using the airfield and obstructions were placed on the field, but now it has 165 flying members and on a busy day there can be as many as thirty gliders in the air at once. The gliders are towed by winch to a height of 1000–1100 ft (305–335 m) before being released. A winch is used because powered aircraft are not allowed by the Peak District Park Authorities, and also the conditions are very windy and are not really suitable for them. The club owns three single-seater and three dual-seater planes. Many of the members have their own aircraft and often these are syndicated, each owner having a quarter share. Members come mostly from Sheffield, Nottingham and South Manchester, although one comes all the way from Glasgow.

The club height record is 23 000 ft (7 000 m), and the distance record stands at 317 miles (510 km).

Eyam Woodlands

The Great Ridge from Castleton

STARTING AND FINISHING POINT
Car-park (110-139827) opposite Speedwell Cavern at the foot of Winnats Pass near Castleton.
LENGTH
8 miles (13 km)
ASCENT
1500 ft (460 m)

The Great Ridge stretches for just two miles from Mam Tor to Lose Hill, giving an aerial view of the vale of Edale on one side and of Hope Valley and Castleton on the other. The walk starts by climbing Winnats Pass, an impressive limestone gorge, and returns beside Peakshole Water, past its source in Castleton where it issues from Peak Cavern, one of several interesting show caves in the village.

ROUTE DESCRIPTION (Maps 19, 20)

From the car-park walk up Winnats Pass *(1)* with the cliffs towering above on either side. At the top of the pass turn R over a stile (PFS). Follow the wall beside the farm and over two stiles to the road. Go straight over the stile opposite and past Windy Knoll Cave on the L, where the bones of Ice Age mammoths were found, to a stile onto the A625. Crossing this, climb up the hillside to a stile onto the road at Mam Nick. Turn immediately R over a stile where a flight of steps, provided by the National Trust to repair the eroded path, is joined leading to the summit of Mam Tor and the Great Ridge *(2)*. At the top of the steps there is a good view of the ramparts of an Iron Age hill fort. Descending from the summit, the remains of the A625 can be seen down on the R. After passing a gate, Hollins Cross is the next low point on the ridge, where an old packhorse route from Castleton to Edale is crossed. Going over two stiles to top the next rise, Back Tor is seen ahead with its almost sheer north-east face. Cross the stile in the dip and climb very steeply up the slope to the top of Back Tor. Lose Hill, the last summit on the Great Ridge, is ½ mile (800 m) further on.

Go over Lose Hill summit. As the path begins to descend, it turns R and goes down the slopes to a double stile. Follow the broad ridge down to a fence and stile. Then at the next stile by a barn, a sunken track is joined, and this leads down to a stile and the lane at Townhead. Turn L and in 300 yards (270 m) join the road to Hope where you turn R, and after ¾ mile (1.2 km) the village of Hope is reached. Going R onto the A625 and then immediately L by the church, take the next R fork (sign 'Pindale'). In a few yards turn R over a stile and follow the river-bank. One stile is met before the single track railway which serves the Hope Cement Works *(3)* is crossed. Take care to watch for any trains. Peakshole Water now veers away from the path which is followed over the fields, crossing three more stiles, until it mets a lane which leads back to the main road.

Turn L onto the road and walk up into Castleton *(4)*. Follow the main road round the S-bend into the main street and then

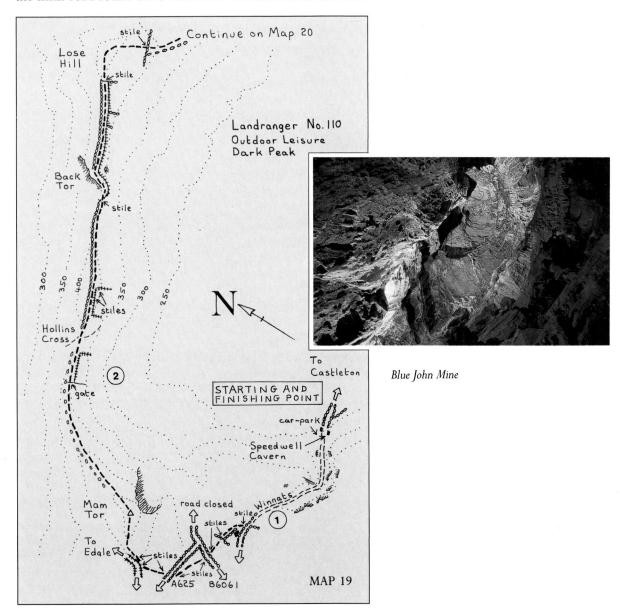

Blue John Mine

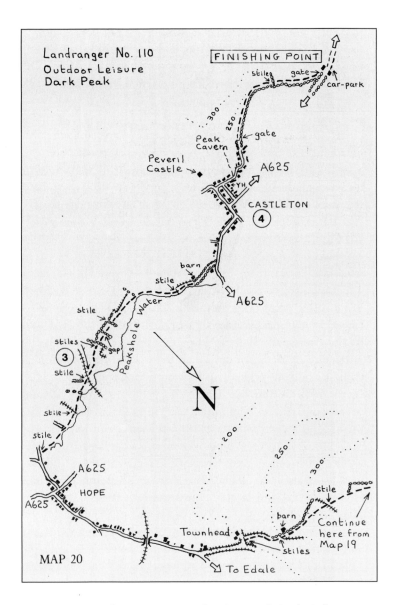

Continue here from Map 19

turn L up Castle Street past the National Park Information Centre. Peveril Castle is seen ahead on the skyline, with the entrance below at the end of the street. It is open all year round. Turn R by the Youth Hostel (sign 'Peak Cavern') and follow the road down to cross Peakshole Water. The footpath on the L leads up to Peak Cavern. Continue along the road, which shortly becomes a track, and go through the gate into the fields. The wall is now followed for ½ mile (800 m), crossing a stile, to arrive at a gate opposite the car-park.

1 Winnats Pass

This narrow road, with a gradient of 1 in 5, climbs between towering limestone cliffs which are best seen on foot rather

Opposite *The Great Ridge from Lose Hill*

than from a car. This old packhorse way and saltway, turnpiked in 1758, was a major highway until the construction in 1817 of a new road round the foot of Mam Tor. However, recent years has seen much more traffic in the pass since the losing battle with landslips led to the closure of the A625 in 1979.

In 1758 a young eloping couple were robbed and murdered in the pass and their bodies thrown into the Speedwell Mine. The saddle of their horse is in the small museum at the Speedwell Mine. Speedwell Mine is open to the public and visitors are taken by boat along an underground canal to the 'Bottomless Pit'.

2 *The Great Ridge*

Mam Tor ('the mother rock') is composed of alternate layers of sandstone and shale, exposed in the great precipice. This is a highly unstable combination which has given rise to Mam Tor's other name, the Shivering Mountain. The summit is ringed by the massive ramparts of an Iron Age fort, cut into by the continually slipping cliff. A packhorse track skirts the north face of Mam Tor, and then follows the ridge to Hollins Cross and down to Hope on the southern slopes of Lose Hill. Until 1633, when a chapel was built at Edale, funeral processions had to climb over the ridge for burial at Hope. Edale Mill, a corn mill, tannery and then a cotton mill, was powered by the River Noe. When it was enlarged in 1795, about 100 women were employed, many of them walking over each day via Hollins Cross from Castleton. The mill closed in 1934 and is now converted into flats.

3 *Hope Cement Works*

Limestone and shale are the essential components of cement and Hope Cement Works, constructed in 1933, is strategically placed at the geological junction of the two. A branch line joins the works to the main railway line over concrete bridges which are quite out of character with the area. The quarry is gradually devouring the limestone to the south and, although providing much needed local employment, limestone quarries and a National Park make uncomfortable companions.

4 *Castleton*

First recorded in 1196, this is essentially a medieval new town. Unlike most mining towns, it was planned, rather than being built by random extensions. Set out under the castle, it ceased to prosper when the castle lost its importance in the fourteenth century. The castle, which was built by William Peveril, William the Conqueror's local bailiff, dates from the eleventh century. The rectangular keep is late Norman of

Looking towards Castleton from Hollins Cross

about 1175. A dry ditch isolates the castle yard, which occupies nearly the whole of the summit, from the rest of the hill. By the seventeenth century the castle was in ruins.

Castleton is famed for its show caves; Speedwell Mine at the foot of Winnats Pass, Treak Cliff Cavern, Blue John Mine, and Peak Cavern, whose entrance, 40 ft (12 m) high and 100 ft (30 m) wide, was once used for rope making. Blue John, which is a blue and yellow coloured fluorspar, is used in the manufacture of ornaments and jewelry which are sold in the local shops.

2·15

KINDER SCOUT FROM HAYFIELD

STARTING AND FINISHING POINT
Car-park on Kinder Road, Hayfield (110-049869).
LENGTH
8 miles (13 km)
ASCENT
1400 ft (430 m)

This is one of the most popular walks from Hayfield. The navigation is relatively easy as the walk sticks mainly to the edge of the Kinder plateau, but it gives the flavour of the wild moorland summit. The highlight of the walk is Kinder Downfall. In hard winters this can freeze to a magnificent wall of ice; while if there is much water in the river and a westerly wind is blowing, the water fails to fall at all and instead is blown upwards, arching back over the edge.

ROUTE DESCRIPTION (Maps 21, 22)

Turn L out of the quarry car-park, where there is a plaque to the Kinder Trespass *(1)*, and walk up Kinder Road for nearly ½ mile (400 m) to the gates of the Water Treatment Works. Turn R over the bridge, follow the farm road for about 50 yards (45 m), then go L (PFS 'KINDER 1') and through a small gate to follow the stream up to the next bridge. Cross this, past the mountain rescue post sign, and go through the small gate opposite. Go up the steep path and follow the wall beside Kinder Reservoir to William Clough.

The path up William Clough *(2)* crosses and recrosses the stream innumerable times. Climb up until you reach the watershed at the top. In front is the start of Ashop Clough which descends to the Snake Road. The three-fingered signpost (PWS) points all ways except the one you should go, which is R and up the steep slopes onto the Kinder Scout plateau. At the top of the steep ascent, turn half R and follow the edge of the plateau. In just under a mile (1.6 km), where the rocks form a cliff, there is a white-painted cross on the rocks nearest the edge, embellished with symbols and the initials G K. This is the sacred spot of the Etherios Society whose leader is George King. Continue along the edge for ½ mile (800 m) to reach Kinder Downfall. If it is in spate you may have to make quite a detour to avoid getting a soaking from the blown back spray.

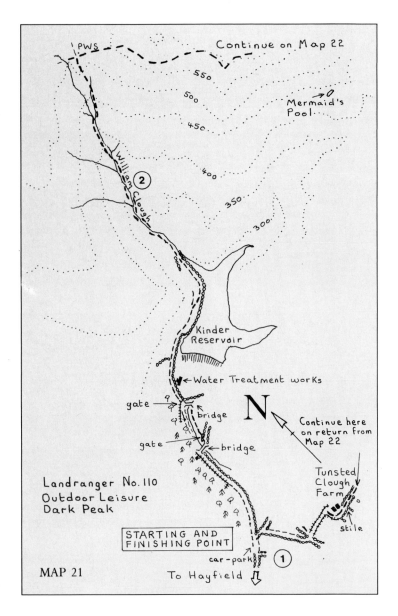

MAP 21

Continue on Map 22

Crossing the River Kinder, continue along the edge now in a southerly direction, meandering through the peat and strangely-eroded boulders, to cross the head of Red Brook in ½ mile (800 m). A similar distance will bring you to the vicinity of Kinder Low. By keeping high up you should see the OS trig point and avoid being diverted down the slopes below Kinderlow End. The OS trig point is only a short way off the path, but can be tricky to find in mist. From Kinderlow there is a good view of Pym Chair on the skyline to the east. Now head just west of south for 300 yards (270 m) to Edale Rocks. Continue past Edale Rocks to drop down to the path which contours round Swine's Back. Ignoring the main eroded path down the hillside, which leads to Brown Knoll, continue contouring round above the wall to meet a ruined sheepfold and then descend by the ruined wall to Edale Cross *(3)*.

Turn R onto the packhorse track and, after following it beside the wall for nearly ½ mile (800 m), turn R over a stile in the wall (PFS 'Hayfield via Tunstead Clough'). The conical-shaped hill to the south is South Head. Follow the path which contours round below Kinderlow End and ignore the L branch which seeks to divert you downhill. In ½ mile (800 m) a gate is reached. Don't go through the gate, but double back to cross a stile on the R. The gate immediately on the L leads to the first of

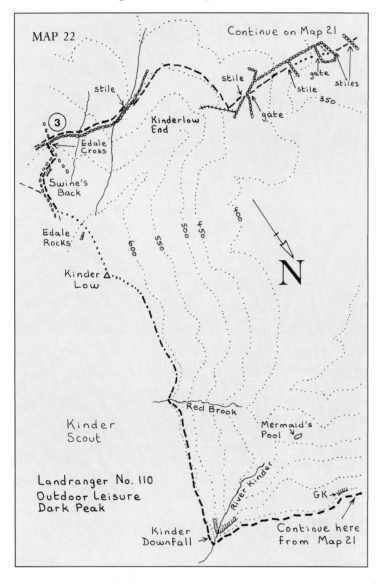

Path on the northern side of Kinder Reservoir

Kinder Reservoir

three fields, which are crossed at stiles and a gate to a main track. Follow the track down to a stile at Tunstead Clough Farm. Go straight ahead on the footpath, not through the farm, and join the farm road. In 250 yards (225 m) turn R onto the road, and walk back down this to Kinder Road and the car-park.

1 Kinder Trespass

For many years Kinder was barred to walkers, being preserved as a grouse moor for the privileged few. On Sunday 24 April 1932 the pent up emotions of the ramblers were released in the celebrated Kinder Scout Mass Trespass. Their intentions had been well advertised in the *Manchester Evening Chronicle* and some 400 people, avoiding the police who were waiting at the planned meeting point in Hayfield, assembled instead in the quarry to hear an address by Benny Rothman, the Mancunian leader of the Trespass. The police who had planned to arrest Benny at the railway station were thwarted when he arrived on his bike.

The Manchester Ramblers Federation opposed the idea of a mass trespass fearing that antagonizing the landowners would hinder rather than promote the cause of access. The walkers, however, set off along the road and up William Clough with the police in close attendance. As they climbed towards the Kinder Scout plateau, gamekeepers appeared and threatened them, but were unable to stop the advance. At the top they were met by more ramblers who had come over from Sheffield and Manchester by other routes, and a victory meeting was held before returning to Hayfield. At Hayfield, Benny and four others were arrested and taken to New Mills, where the next day they were charged with unlawful assembly and breach of the peace. Committed to the Derby Assizes on 21/22 July, they were found guilty of riotous assembly and Benny Rothman was sentenced to four months in prison.

The publicity, however, had made the public aware of the situation and restrictions were gradually lessened until in 1951 the formation of the Peak District National Park opened up the area with the negotiation of Access Agreements with the landowners. Now 76 square miles (19,684 hectares) of moorland are open to the public all year round, except for a few days each year kept for grouse shooting.

2 *William Clough*

The stream which tumbles down little waterfalls makes this a very pleasant approach to Kinder Scout (from the Saxon 'Kyndwr Scut' meaning 'water over the edge'). The stream, usually small but which after heavy rain becomes a torrent, has cut down through the peat exposing the layers of underlying shale and gritstone. The harder gritstone resists erosion and so causes the stream to flow in these pretty falls. Towards the top of the clough there is a thick deposit of clay covering the underlying rocks. This was formed in very cold conditions towards the end of the Ice Age. The runnels and scars are the work of water erosion.

3 *Edale Cross*

Recently protected and almost enclosed by a stone wall, this stone pillar in the shape of a cross is also called Champion Cross from 'Champayne' which was the name for the southern part of Peak Forest in the Middle Ages. The forest wards of Longdendale, Ashop, Edale and Champayne met near here, and such points were usually marked by a stone. This was an old medieval road and later a packhorse way. The initials J. G. and the date 1810 inscribed on the cross are much later and refer to restoration work.

2·16

SHUTLINGSLOE AND MACCLESFIELD FOREST

STARTING AND FINISHING POINT
Lay-by at Trentabank Reservoir near Macclesfield (118-963711).
LENGTH
8 miles (13 km)
ASCENT
1700 ft (520 m)

This very attractive walk on the edge of the Peak District starts from a heronry, visits Shutlingsloe (the 'Cheshire Matterhorn'), and climbs through the charming Cumberland Clough to visit one of the highest inns in England.

ROUTE DESCRIPTION (Maps 23, 24)

A stile leads straight into the forest from opposite the lay-by and the climb starts immediately among the cool shade of the pines. Water Board signs discourage deviation from the path which is followed to a stile at the forest edge and then out onto the moor. Topping the rise ahead, the summit cone of Shutlingsloe (once known as Scyttel's Hill) is seen. The boggiest part of the moor is crossed by a board walk, which certainly keeps you out of the mud, but is not the happiest solution to the erosion problem. Turn R over the stile and follow the wall to the ladder stile below the summit. A short, but steep ascent brings you to the OS trig point and an expansive view of the moors ahead beyond Wildboarclough *(1)*.

The path down over the rocks from the summit is waymarked to lead round Shutlingsloe Farm over two stiles to the farm road. Go down this a short way and turn L on the lower path which, passing Banktop, follows the edge of the wood and over two stiles to join the road at a very high ladder stile. Cross this and the narrow bridge opposite, and go through a gate by the barn into the farmyard. Go straight across the road to a gate and follow Cumberland Brook, first on the R bank, and then over a bridge and up the L bank through another gate. A few pine trees line the brook until the path forks at the top gate. Follow the L branch, passing a waterfall, and out onto the open moor. The path continues on the L side of the clough, only crossing to the R near the top. Turn L at the PFS to reach the Cat and Fiddle Inn *(2)* in under a mile (1.6 km).

Turn L on the A537, and at the L bend take the track known

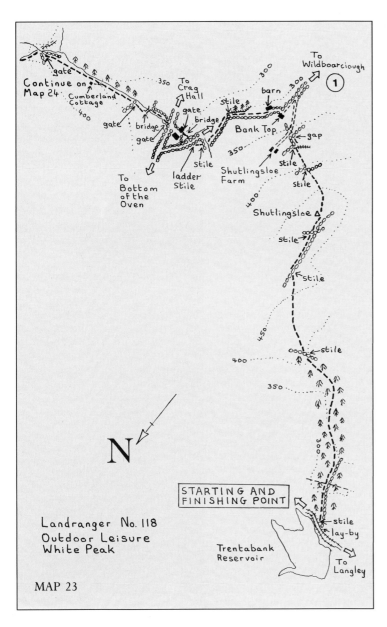

To Wildboarclough

①

barn

350 · · To Crag
300
Hall

Continue on
Map 24
Cumberland
Cottage
400

stile

gate

gate

bridge

gate

bridge

gate

Bank Top

gap

350

350

stile

stile

Shutlingsloe
Farm

stile

To
Bottom
of the
Oven

ladder
Stile

stile

400

Shutlingsloe △

stile

stile

stile

450

stile

400

350

300

N

STARTING AND
FINISHING POINT

Landranger No. 118
Outdoor Leisure
White Peak

Trentabank
Reservoir

stile
lay-by

To
Langley

MAP 23

as Stoneyway *(3)* across the moor and down to the Shining Tor
Restaurant. Cross the main road and follow the minor road to
reach the Stanley Arms in a mile (1.6 km). Turn L and then R at
the fork in 200 yards (180 m). A narrow packway (Oven Lane)
between walls on the R leads up to Forest Chapel *(4)*. Go
straight ahead down the road to the forest edge (PFS) and turn L
over the stile. The path leads downhill through the trees and
past a small pool to arrive at the road at a stile. Turn R and
follow this back to Trentabank Reservoir.

Macclesfield Forest

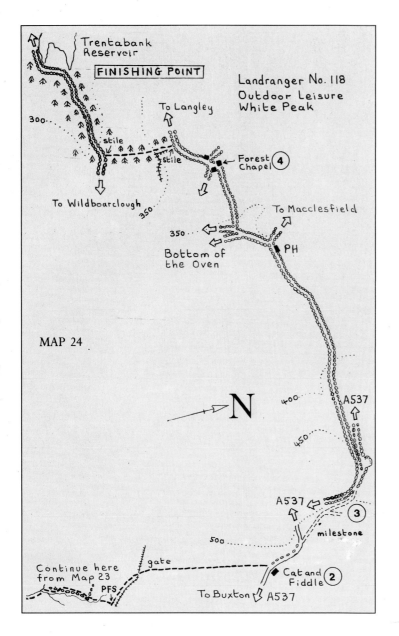

MAP 24

1 Wildboarclough

Until recently no less than three mills stood by this little cluster of houses. The first, built in the mid-eighteenth century, employed a contractor to manufacture the machinery, and he had one James Brindley working for him. One Sunday, Brindley walked to Manchester to study the mill on which the Wildboarclough Mill was to be based. Being illiterate, he memorized the details of its construction before returning to complete the installation. Brindley, of course,

Hills between Forest Chapel and Shining Tor

went on to become the foremost engineer of his generation. A further two mills were built, employing a total of 600 workers; and these were used as silk mills, then later for carpets. In 1958 the mills were demolished leaving only one building remaining, which, until recently, was used as what must have been the biggest sub-post office in the country. The imposing Crag Hall at the top of the village belongs to Lord Derby.

The area has been a royal hunting forest from medieval times, but if indeed as local history claims the last wild boar in England was killed here, then it must have had more lives than a cat, as it has been exterminated in several other places as well.

2 *Cat and Fiddle Inn*

Built early in the eighteenth century, this is the second highest inn in England (the highest is Tan Hill in Yorkshire). The origin of the name is rather obscure and is variously attributed to Catherine le Fidele, the wife of Czar Peter the Great; or to a Duke of Devonshire who is reputed to have stopped here to play his fiddle; or, rather more probably, to the game of 'Cat', the fiddle being for dancing. There is a carving of a cat and fiddle on the front of the inn. During the winter when the road is often blocked by snow, the inn sometimes becomes an involuntary overnight halt for travellers.

3 *Stoneyway*

This is an early turnpike of 1759, 30 ft (9 m) wide and surfaced with small stones retained between banks. A little way along it is an old milestone showing 'LONDON 164 MACCLESFIELD 6'. The turnpike passed behind the site of the inn and descended to Goyt's Clough. A new turnpike on the route of the present road, which passes in front of the inn, was made in 1821.

4 *Forest Chapel*

This little church of St Stephen continues the ancient tradition of rush bearing and the ceremony is held in mid-August. Rushes taken from the moor are strewn on the floor of the decorated church, as they were when this was the only form of floor covering. The church, with its tower, built in 1673 and rebuilt in 1834, was used as a set in the filming of the TV series 'The Jewel in the Crown'. In the church porch is a list of thirty-seven different varieties of plant which can be found in the churchyard, and an addendum lists another thirty-two to be found nearby.

LATHKILL AND BRADFORD DALES

STARTING AND FINISHING POINT
Moor Lane car-park near Youlgreave (119-194645).
LENGTH
10 miles (16 km) or 8 miles (13 km) variant
ASCENT
700 ft (210 m)

From its upper, narrow, dry limestone gorge, through the Derbyshire Dales Nature Reserve, where the river rises, to the green depths of the pools towards Alport, Lathkill Dale has always something of interest to see. At one time this tranquil valley was the centre of a major mining enterprise, with shafts and levels, waterwheels and aqueducts. The scene now is one of woods and flowers with the river flowing peacefully past, while the return along the River Bradford passes wide, deep pools where fish lie still in the depths.

Upper Lathkill Dale

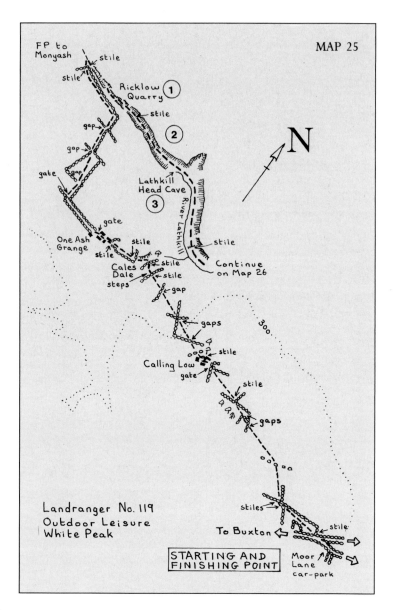

ROUTE DESCRIPTION (Maps 25–27)

From the car-park turn L up to the road junction and over the stile opposite. The waymarked path goes through a gap in the wall and then over two stiles at the corner of the next field. Head for the PFS at the ruined wall and turn half L towards the trees. At the next gap turn half R and then through a gap into the wood. Leaving the wood at a stile in about 50 yards (45 m), go towards Calling Low Farm where a gate leads into the farmyard. Go through two gates in the yard and a stile on the R beyond the farm which leads to open fields. These are followed downhill through three gaps to a stile above Cales Dale. A flight

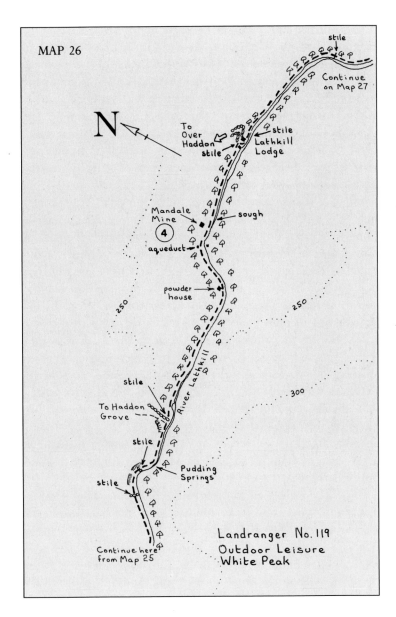

MAP 26

N

To Over Haddon
stile
stile
Lathkill Lodge
Continue on Map 27
stile

Mandale Mine
④
sough
aqueduct

powder house

River Lathkill

250

250

300

stile
To Haddon Grove

stile

Pudding Springs

stile

Continue here from Map 25

Landranger No. 119
Outdoor Leisure
White Peak

of 120 steep steps leads down into the bottom of the dale.

At the bottom, go over the stile where the walk may be shortened by a couple of miles by turning R down to Lathkill Dale. The longer route climbs ahead and then L (PFS 'Limestone Way') to cross a stile into a field, and then over high stone steps into the farmyard at One Ash Grange just to the L of a barn. Go through the yard and turn R by the camping barn to a gate onto the farm road which is followed up to a gate at the end on the R. The path now crosses four fields and turns L to descend to meet the head of Lathkill Dale at a stone stile. Turn sharp R over a wooden stile and walk down the dale, which rapidly narrows beneath Ricklow Quarry *(1)*.

Reaching a stile, Lathkill Dale Nature Reserve *(2)* is now entered where the rare flower Jacob's Ladder may be found. In ½ mile (800 m), the obvious opening of Lathkill Head Cave *(3)* appears on the R and on the L is Parson's Tor, named after the Rector of Monyash who fell from the top with his horse in 1776 while returning in the snow after preaching at Bakewell. The junction with Cales Dale soon appears at a footbridge on the R. The waterfall of Pudding Springs ½ mile (800 m) further, tumbles over tufa beds, and then, at the site of Carter's Mill, the path enters ash woodland at a stile.

Signs of mining can be seen all down the valley for the next mile (1.6 km). Shortly after the pillars of the aqueduct, Mandale Mine *(4)* appears on the L with the sough just beside the path. A minor road is reached at a stile by Lathkill Lodge. Turn R and then L to pass the lodge. A further mile (1.6 km) beside wide fish pools (which have been artificially improved by weirs) will bring you to Conksbury Bridge. Turn R across the bridge on the old Grindleford turnpike, and a few yards up the hill turn L at a stile, now on the other side of the river. The path follows a fence and wall, crossing four stiles to Raper Lodge, where a small road is crossed. To the L is Coalpit Bridge, over which packhorses carried coal from Chesterfield. Continue beside a wall through eight fields to Alport, where the main road is joined at the bridge which dates from 1793. The Old Portway, an ancient trackway, forded the Lathkill at this point. The pretty village of Alport, with its attractive gardens, corn mill and old bridges, makes a pleasant detour.

Cross the main road and follow the track (PFS 'Middleton by Youlgreave') over the River Bradford and through a squeezer stile by a gate. The track runs beside the river to join another track just after a stile. Follow this track beside the river to a road and continue, now on the R bank. (In 1881 the River Bradford disappeared down a large hole caused by the collapse of old mine workings and reappeared at Darley Dale.) A ¼ mile (400 m) further at a stile, a flat stone slab bridge is crossed back to the L bank and through a small gate. Walk beside the river with its fish pools for ½ mile (800 m) to a small gate and turn R over the bridge. A track zig-zags up the hillside to the road. Turn R on the road, past Lomberdale Hall, and then L over the stile at the road bend to cross a field to a stile onto the higher road. Do not take the footpath opposite, but go L and then R over the next stile in a few yards where a clear waymarked path slants uphill across the field. At the third stile turn R, and follow the wall which leads back to Moor Lane car-park.

Lathkill Dale

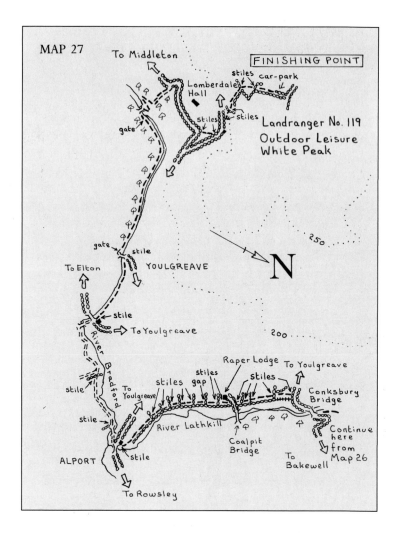

1 *Ricklow Quarry*

The tips of the old marble mine have cascaded into the dale by an old mine entrance. The marble, a crinoidal limestone, was extracted from these workings until their collapse in 1900. The cave, a natural fissure, was enlarged by miners attempting to drain the Magpie Mine on Sheldon Moor, who after a short way found it intersected with a natural cavern. The short passage ends in a 15 ft (4.5 m) pitch, the total length of the cave being 250 ft (75 m). The date 1787 and the initials of Isaac Berresford (the miner who, together with his son, dug the Ricklow level) are carved at the entrance.

2 *Lathkill Dale Nature Reserve*

The dale, for so long ringing to the sounds of industry, is now a Derbyshire Dales Nature Reserve, managed by the Nature Conservancy Council; and the only noise comes from the visitors and the 10000 school and university students who come to study here every year. The native ash woodland has been actively managed from the eleventh century, and the river is claimed to be the purest in the country.

3 *Lathkill Head Cave*

If it has been wet weather the river may be flowing from the cave, but more usually it is dry and the river emerges further down the dale. The entrance, about 20 ft (6 m) high, soon closes down to a flat out crawl of 200 ft (60 m). The total length of the cave is 2000 ft (610 m), all of which floods in wet weather. Directly opposite, behind a bush, is Critchlow Cave which has 500 ft (150 m) of passages.

4 *Mandale Mine*

This is one of the oldest mines in Derbyshire having been worked from the thirteenth century and possibly from as far back as Roman times. Water has always been a problem with the mine. In 1798 the Mandale Mine Company started to drive the Mandale Sough, a task which took over thirty years. The sough can be seen where it emerges under the path and drains into the river. As this proved inadequate, pumping was found to be necessary and a 35 ft (10.5 m) diameter waterwheel was installed in 1840 for the purpose. The leat can be traced back along the hillside to the pillars of the aqueduct, which was constructed to carry the water across the river from the leat on the other side. The wheel pumped water out of the mine from a depth of 90 ft (27 m). In 1848 a Cornish beam engine was installed to improve the drainage of the mine, but the effort was in vain and the mine closed in 1851. The end wall of the engine house still stands and close by is the shaft which has been capped. The two small openings by the path are abandoned trial levels where no lead ore was found. On no account should mines be entered as there can be unstable rocks and hidden shafts.

Near Monyash

Saddleworth Moor and the Four Reservoirs

STARTING AND FINISHING
POINT
Car-park at Dove Stones
Reservoir east of Greenfield
(110-014035).
LENGTH
9½ miles (15 km)
ASCENT
1000 ft (300 m)

On sunny weekends the chain of reservoirs from Greenfield, through Yeoman Hey, to Dove Stone, with its myriad sails of small boats, is an attraction which brings many people to stroll round the shores. Less frequented and much wilder are the rocky edges and the moors above, where it is difficult to realize that Manchester and city streets are so close at hand.

Route Description (Maps 28, 29)

Go down Bradbury Lane to the L of the Ranger Briefing Centre to pass Forty Row Cottages *(1)* on the R in about ¼ mile (400 m). The road then becomes a cobbled track and continues to Fern Lea ½ mile (800 m) further. Double back on the higher track which climbs gradually to reach, and then enter, a coniferous wood at a stile. The path goes through the wood and comes again to open land, crossing two stiles and streams before entering the mainly deciduous Chew Piece Plantation at the third stile. Leaving the wood, the impressive rocks on the skyline to the R are Wimberry Rocks or Indian's Head. The track, which is that of the Chew Valley Tramway *(2)*, continues for ½ mile (800 m) to cross the stream at the site of the old bridge. The National Park Authority is planning to replace this bridge as the stream can be difficult to cross when in spate.

Climb up the hillside opposite to join the road and turn R. You can scramble up beside the stream, but it is advisable to join the road which leads up to the Chew Reservoir *(3)* before the gorge gets too difficult. Turn L along the dam, and at the far end take the path to the L across the moor, heading due west roughly parallel to the edge. In ¼ mile (400 m) join the edge at the Dish Stone. Follow this for 1¼ miles (2 km), past the rocks of Charnel Holes and then the remains of a shooting cabin,

Dove Stone and Yeoman Hey Reservoirs from the north

Bramley's Cot, tucked in by the rocks, to reach Fox Stone with its prominent cairn in memory of Brian Toase and Tom Moreton, two rock climbers who were killed in the Italian Dolomites.

In ½ mile (800 m) cross two deeply cut cloughs by a detour and then head for the memorial cross erected to the unfortunate Member of Parliament for Oldham, James Platt, who was killed here in a shooting accident in 1857. Major's Cairn, named after a dog, is to the R of the path. The next objective, Raven Stones, the last reported site of a nesting golden eagle in Yorkshire, is on the very edge, so descend to the lip of the plateau. The striking pillar of rock, isolated from the adjacent cliff, is known as the Trinnacle. The ascent of its topmost prong is not particularly difficult, but requires a steady nerve.

Go directly down the hillside to the L of the Trinnacle (no path and rather steep), and cross the low wall to join the valley

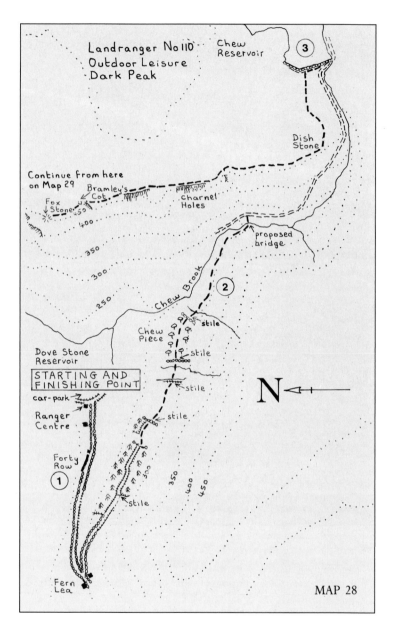

MAP 28

track by the entrance to the water tunnel *(4)*. The track leads down to Greenfield Reservoir *(5)* and alongside it to the dam. Crossing the leat below the dam at a bridge, go down to the footbridge beneath the dam. A new footpath now follows the south bank of the stream past the old dynamite hut, now a refuge, and along the Yeoman Hey Reservoir *(6)* to join a road at the dam. In 300 yards (270 m) at the bridge go through the gate on the L and over a stile. Follow the fence above Dove Stone Reservoir *(7)* for nearly a mile (1.6 km) through a gate and over two stiles, until the path forks R descending to the stream at a bridge. From here the road leads to the car-park.

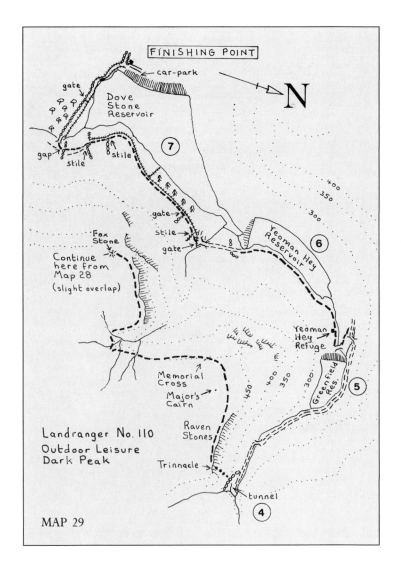

MAP 29

Fletchers paper mill

1 *Forty Row Cottages*

In fact now only half that number, as the original back-to-back cottages have been combined. The cottages were built for the mill workers at Fletchers paper mill below, which produces a very fine type of paper.

2 *Chew Valley Tramway*

During the building of the Chew Reservoir (1907–1914), this railway was constructed to carry the clay which was required to waterproof the reservoir. The clay came from near the Roaches Inn at Mossley and was hauled along the 4 miles (6 km) of 3 ft (90 cm) gauge line by steam trains.

3 *Chew Reservoir*

Completed in 1912 and when full containing 206 million gallons, this is claimed to be the highest reservoir in England, being 1600 ft (488 m) in altitude.

4 Water Tunnel

When the waters of the north-western moors were channelled into the newly built Yeoman Hey Reservoir in 1880, there were vociferous objections from the local mill owners. Not only were they being deprived of water for their mills, but, to add insult to injury, the water was theirs by right as the Water Board didn't actually own the moors from which it was being taken. The tunnel, ¾ mile (1.2 km) long, was built by the Water Board to divert this misappropriated water into a leat which bypasses the reservoir below. The tunnel is sometimes almost dry, but in flood conditions can fill nearly to the roof, and the power of the water thundering forth from the end of the tunnel is awe inspiring.

5 Greenfield Reservoir

Greenfield Reservoir, the highest and smallest of a chain of three reservoirs, was constructed in 1903. The complicated flood gates at the dam were built in 1982 as insurance against possible, but unlikely, extreme flood conditions. Should this happen, the concrete gates would open allowing the water to flow away.

6 Yeoman Hey Reservoir

Built in 1880, and the cause of all the trouble at t'mill, Yeomen Hey Reservoir can contain 206 million gallons of rather peaty water. The peat is removed at the Greenfield Treatment Works below by means of sand filters through which the water is forced under pressure.

7 Dove Stone Reservoir

The latest and very recent addition to the trio of reservoirs, Dove Stone Reservoir was completed in 1967 and holds 1110 million gallons. It is used primarily as compensation water and also supplies Fletchers paper mill which is presently taking about 3½ million gallons a day, but it can also supply drinking water by pumping the water into the Yeoman Hey Reservoir above whose output goes to the filtration plant.

Dove Stone Moss from the Ranger Briefing Centre

2·19

BACK TOR AND LADYBOWER RESERVOIR

STARTING AND FINISHING
POINT
Lay-by on the Snake Road (A57)
near the Ladybower Reservoir
(110-196864).
LENGTH
10 miles (16 km)
ASCENT
1200 ft (370 m)

This walk along the high moorland above Ladybower Reservoir is approached by an attractive, quiet path through the trees behind the Ladybower Inn and up to the sinisterly named Cutthroat Bridge. Along the edge frequent rocky tors provide interest and vantage points for views of the reservoirs below, until Lost Lad is reached which is the turning point. The following quiet stretch of moorland then brings you down to Ladybower to join the popular walk beside the reservoir.

ROUTE DESCRIPTION (Maps 30, 31)

From the lay-by go L and take the private road on the R, just before the viaduct, which in a few yards turns to the R uphill. In about 200 yards (180 m) the road becomes a track and goes through a gate, and then another smaller gate onto a wide grassy path through the bracken. Proceed along this path for ¼ mile (400 m), with Ladybower Reservoir *(1)* below on the R, to a gate above the Ladybower Inn. A track from the inn on the main road is joined and followed uphill to enter the Nature Reserve at a gate. The clear path is followed for ¾ mile (1.2 km) crossing a small stream and through a gate until Highshaw Clough is reached at Cutthroat Bridge. The bridge is named after a man who was found there with his throat cut in 1635.

The path now follows the stream uphill a short way and then bears L, gradually climbing across the moor with Win Hill across the valley to the L. After 1 mile (1.6 km) over the heather-clad moorland the edge is reached with a sudden breathtaking view of Ladybower Reservoir spread out below. Turn R and walk uphill towards the rocks of Whinstone Lee Tor. This is an excellent viewpoint, with the tempting Bleaklow wilderness stretching away into the northern distance.

The path now goes north-east, passing the Hurkling Stones on the R and crossing the Moscar path in ½ mile (800 m), before turning north for Wheel Stones ¼ mile (400 m) further

Opposite Ladybower Reservoir from the west side

118

Back Tor

on. Passing this isolated tor, fork R over White Tor in ¼ mile (400 m), where, looking back at the Wheel Stones, it is clear why it has acquired its other name of the Coach and Horses. After a similar distance, the Salt Cellar stands proudly on the edge. A further mile (1.6 km) of easy walking, passing Dovestone Tor and the Cakes of Bread, brings you to the Abbey Grange to Strines path. Back Tor with its OS trig point, which it is quite awkward to attain, is then 250 yards (225 m) beyond.

From Back Tor head north-west across the moor to Lost Lad *(2)*, where there is a cairn, and continue to a path which turns off westwards downhill to join a wider path. Turn L, and then in 200 yards (180 m) L again to head south-west towards Lose Hill in the distance and across the moor to a broken wall with a ladder stile beyond. The path now goes steeply downhill, with Ladybower Reservoir again in view ahead, to turn L onto a path which follows the hillside. Cross the fence at a ladder stile and past ruined walls to a small cluster of pine trees. Follow the ruined wall for ½ mile (800 m), and at a sign 'No Access' go half L downhill to a ladder stile. Through a gap in the next wall and the path becomes a track which descends to Lanehead Cottage. Go through the gate into a green lane and follow this downhill over a couple of stiles to join the road at the reservoir.

Turn L on the road to cross Mill Brook which once ran down to the now drowned village of Derwent *(3)*, and follow the road for a little under 2 miles (3.2 km) beside the reservoir back to the starting point.

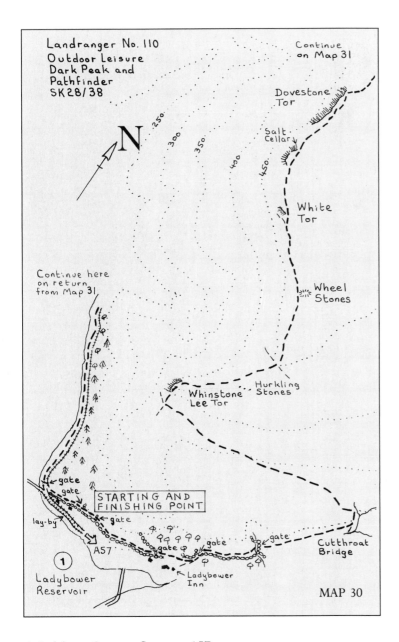

1 *Ladybower Reservoir* See page 157

2 *Lost Lad*

The cairn marks the place where the body of a young shepherd boy was found one spring in the sixteenth century by a shepherd who noticed writing on the rocks. It is said the words 'Lost Lad' were scratched on the rock by the boy who had become lost in a winter blizzard while gathering sheep.

3 *Derwent Village*

The small, historic, farming village of Derwent, with its church, cottages and hall, as well as ten farmhouses, disappeared beneath the waters of the Ladybower Reservoir

121

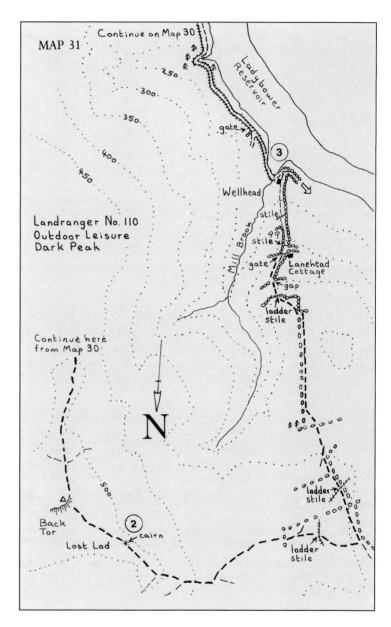

Moorland near the Cakes of Bread

in 1946. The valley roads were reconstructed, two large viaducts built, and the villagers were rehoused at Yorkshire Bridge. For a year the spire of the 1867 Anglican church still stood above the water, but was then demolished for safety. This church superseded the original chapel built in 1757. The hall, built in 1672 by Lord of the Manor, Henry Balguy, was extended to accommodate shooting parties, and a private chapel was also built. From 1920 until its closure in 1943, the hall was used as a youth hostel. Occasionally in dry summers the sad remains of the village emerge briefly above the water.

THE ROACHES, LUD'S CHURCH AND GIB TORR

STARTING AND FINISHING POINT
Lay-by on the road between Upper Hulme, near Leek, and Roach End (119-004621).
LENGTH
10 miles (16 km)
ASCENT
1400 ft (430 m)

The Roaches and Back Forest, with the mysterious depths of Lud's Church, those strangest of naturalized English creatures – the wallabies–and one of the highest gritstone outcrops in the Peak, form a microcosm of all that is best in this area.

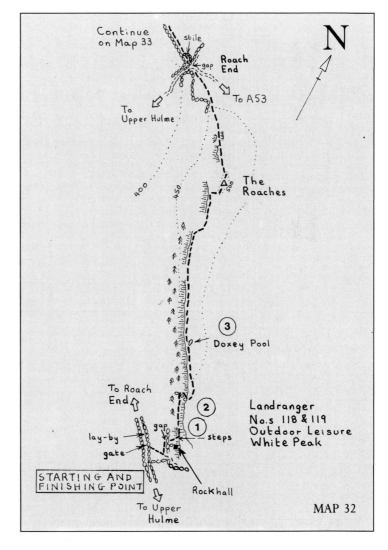

MAP 32

Moorland and gritstone, heather and bilberries, the call of the lark overhead, remind one of the quiet beauty of the northern moors. Yet the Roaches are so close to the road that on summer evenings the crags are busy with climbers enjoying some of the longest climbs in the Peak.

ROUTE DESCRIPTION (Maps 32–35)

Go through the gate next to the lay-by and follow the track towards the rocks with the slopes of Hen Cloud on the R ('Cloud' is from the Celtic 'clud' meaning 'hill'). Turn L and skirt Rockhall Cottage to turn R through a gap in the wall. A flight of rock steps leads up through the lower crags. These steps are the steepest and probably the hardest part of the walk! At the top on the L, perched on the edge of the vertical drop, is a gritstone boulder in the form of a seat or throne *(1)*, and on the R is the Great Slab *(2)*. Walk along the terrace and, on emerging from the trees, turn R along a broken wall. Ascend through a gap in the upper tier of rocks and at the top is moorland with fine views towards Ramshaw Rocks. Turn L

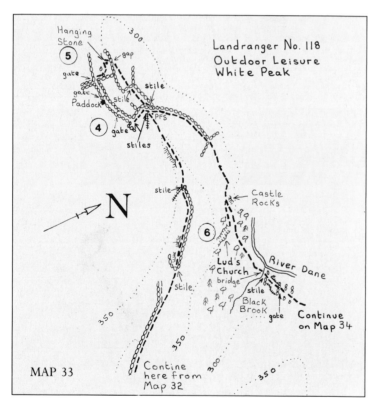

MAP 33

The Roaches

along a clear path and Doxey Pool *(3)* is soon reached. Continue along the ridge to the summit of the Roaches.

Descending from the summit to the road at Roach End, squeeze through the gap in the wall opposite and over a stile to follow the broad ridge of Back Forest. When the wall veers off to the L, continue on the concessionary path along the ridge. Cross the stile in the next wall and stay on the ridge, crossing another stile, until the path descends to meet a crossroads (PFS). Turn L over the stile towards Swythamley Hall *(4)* then R at the stile. Follow the lane which leads through two gates, passing Paddock Farm, until it turns L at a gate. Turn R on the concessionary footpath which is signed to Hanging Stone on the hill above. Ascend the rock steps on the L of Hanging Stone *(5)*,

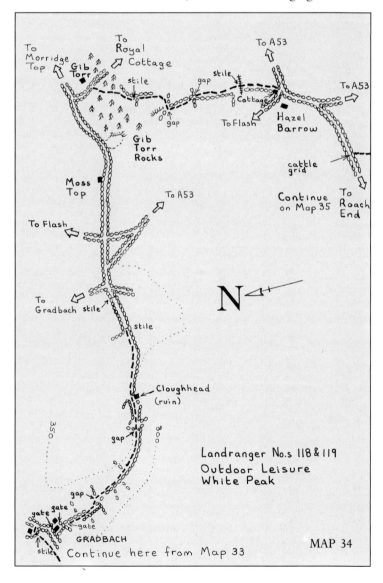

through a gap, and follow the path over the fields and three stiles to the Gradbach signpost.

The path soon enters woodland of silver birch, oak and rowan, and arrives at Castle Rocks where a carved stone points the way to Lud's Church *(6)*. After exploring this, return to Castle Rocks and double back R to descend to where the River Dane meets Black Brook. Cross Black Brook by the bridge and, just uphill from the bridge, cross the wall on the L to follow a rising track through a gate and over the fields to a stile at the farm, which belongs to the Buxton and District Scouts. Turn R from the farmyard onto a road and in a few yards L again through a gate beside a farm. Passing through the farmyard and two gates follow a slightly sunken path, first on the R of the wall and then on the L. The prominent rock on the skyline to the L is called the Yawning Stone.

Make for the tumbledown Cloughhead Cottage by a tree and follow a rising track on the L side of the valley. At the top of the rise the view opens out with Gib Torr, the next objective, straight ahead. After two stiles, on emerging onto the road, note the unusual sign 'GRADBACH NOT ROACH END'. The depressions on the moor ahead are the remains of old coal pits. Keeping straight ahead, after ¾ mile (1.2 km) turn R and descend to Gib Torr Farm, just past which an unsigned path enters the woods on the R. On leaving the trees, pass through a stile and, avoiding the worst of the bog, make for just L of the huge gritstone tor on the skyline. Turn L through a gap and follow the ridge to a stile, and then emerge at the junction of three roads by a cottage.

Take the road opposite the cottage and then the R fork after

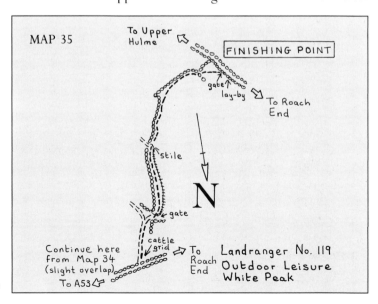

MAP 35

To Upper Hulme

FINISHING POINT

gate
lay-by

To Roach End

stile

N

gate

cattle grid

Continue here from Map 34 (slight overlap)

To Roach End

Landranger No. 119
Outdoor Leisure
White Peak

To A53

the surprisingly situated Hazel Barrow (tropical) Fish Farm. In ¼ mile (400 m) turn L at a cattle grid and follow the track to re-enter the Roaches Estate at a gate. When the track turns L, go over the stile to reach open moorland again. Cresting a slight rise, Hen Cloud reappears in view with Tittesworth Reservoir beyond. Descending the old pre-turnpike road, pass between Hen Cloud and the Roaches and walk down the track to the road.

1 *Gritstone Seat*

A throne is appropriate enough, for this was once the scene of a royal visit. A plaque nearby records 'Visited by the Prince and Princess of Teck August 23rd 1872'. The Princess of Teck was Queen Mary's mother and now, over a hundred years later, the area has passed into the hands of the Peak Park Board who bought it in 1980 for the sum of £185 000 after access difficulties had threatened this delightful area.

2 *Great Slab*

The Great Slab and the overhang above it is the route of the late Don Whillans' sensational climb, 'Sloth', which ascends directly over the overhang. On the face of the Great Slab is the Pedestal on which climbers may be seen summoning up courage to attempt the Sloth overhang, or perhaps on one of the easier routes which avoid the difficulties.

3 *Doxey Pool*

In summer this is a rippled pool set among heather, bilberry and cotton grass; in winter it can sometimes become a solid block of ice over which one walks almost without seeing it. There are no streams flowing into the pool, and it comes as something of a surprise to find that the summit of the Roaches is not far away, nor very much higher. Doxey Pool is supposedly named after the daughter of Bess Bowyer who lived at Rockhall and was herself the daughter of a highwayman.

4 *Swythamley Hall*

This was once the home of Sir Philip Brocklehurst, and it was from here that the most famous of the Roaches' inhabitants came. A private zoo based at the hall released the wallabies which still roam the woods of Back Forest. Although the wallabies have been depleted in numbers by harsh winters, attempts have been made in recent years to maintain the stock by releasing others to join them. Their continued survival seems rather precarious, but by walking quietly and watching carefully, for they are so well camouflaged that unless they move it is difficult to see them, you may well take home a very special memory of the Roaches. Please leave

Rockhall

them to live quietly and do not disturb them, or in future years, like the herd of deer which once also were to be seen here, they may all have gone forever.

5 *Hanging Stone*

On one face of the Hanging Stone there is a memorial to Lt. Col. Henry Courtney Brocklehurst. On the opposite face an older testimonial reads:

> Beneath this rock
> August 1, 1874 was buried
> BURKE
> A Noble Mastiff
> Black and Tan
> Faithful as woman
> Braver than man
> A gun and a ramble
> His heart's desire
> With the friend of his life
> The Swythamley Squire

6 *Lud's Church*

This is much easier to find since the Peak Park Board have taken control of the area, but it was at one time a safe haven for the Lollards who worshipped here. A short distance along the path from Castle Rocks a narrow entrance on the R leads you to a flight of steps descending into the bottom of Lud's Church. This chasm, about 50 ft (15 m) deep, has been caused by a landslip of gigantic proportions, and the main fault is visible for some distance beyond Lud's Church. The name Lud's Church is from the fourteenth-century pastor Walter de Lud-auk, whose grand-daughter is supposed to have been buried nearby after being killed in a raid by the King's troops.

129

BLEAKLOW FROM GLOSSOP

STARTING AND FINISHING
POINT
Old Glossop. Cars may be parked
beside factory (110-045948) on the
north-east outskirts of Glossop.
LENGTH
10 miles (16 km)
ASCENT
1450 ft (450 m)

There are three summits in the Peak District which achieve the magic height of 2000 ft (610 m) and two of these, Bleaklow Head and Higher Shelf Stones, are visited on this walk. The strangely eroded shapes of Wain Stones, Hern Stones and Higher Shelf Stones on the high moors have attracted walkers for over a hundred years.

The ascent, up Torside Clough, along the Pennine Way, and the descent, down the reputed Roman road of Doctor's Gate, both follow good footpaths beside clear, sparkling mountain streams. This ascent of Bleaklow is both delightful and much easier underfoot than many of the alternative routes.

ROUTE DESCRIPTION (Maps 36–38)

From the parking place, turn L at the end of the factory and follow the road round until it meets Charles Lane, which doubles back up the hill to a stile. Passing a quarry the sunken lane goes uphill through three stiles to a fourth where the walls fan out. Turn half L following the L wall, and in 250 yards (225 m) strike directly up the hillside to a stile in the fence. A bearing of NE brings you to Glossop Low Quarries (1), a complex array of depressions and spoil heaps through which you should attempt to navigate a straight line to arrive at the OS trig point on the top of Cock Hill.

From the summit walk for about ½ mile (800 m) still on a NE bearing over rough grass and heather until a stony track is reached. Turn R along it to the ruined shooting cabin on Glossop Low. From the ruin follow a faint path, again heading NE, and in a few yards the Woodlands Valley comes into view. On the skyline are the twin Holme Moss television masts, and opposite can be seen Crowden Youth Hostel in the valley of Crowden Brook, which is for many walkers the end of a long, first day on the Pennine Way. The path leads across the moor for ¼ mile (400 m) until, quite suddenly and dramatically,

Opposite The Pennine Way looking towards Higher Shelf Stones

Torside Clough appears at your feet. The Pennine Way is joined at this point.

Turn R and follow Clough Edge on a level path, with the clough gradually climbing to meet it. After a mile (1.6 km) Wildboar Grain joints Torside Clough. Turn L, descending to cross the stream, and follow the path eastwards up the L bank. In ¾ mile (1.2 km), where the stream gradually disappears and the peat groughs become more evident, the path swings gradually R. Continue along the path and after a further ¼ mile (400 m) the cairn on Bleaklow Head is reached, surrounded by a sea of silver sand.

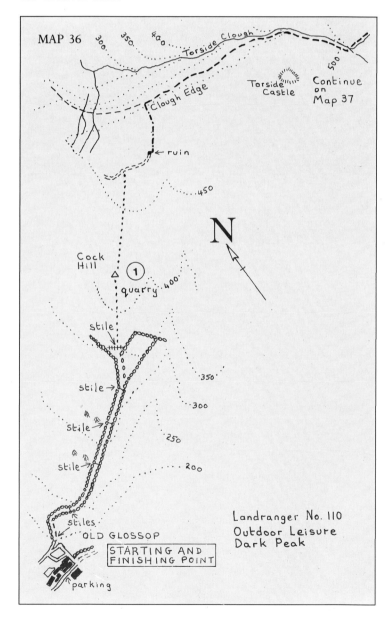

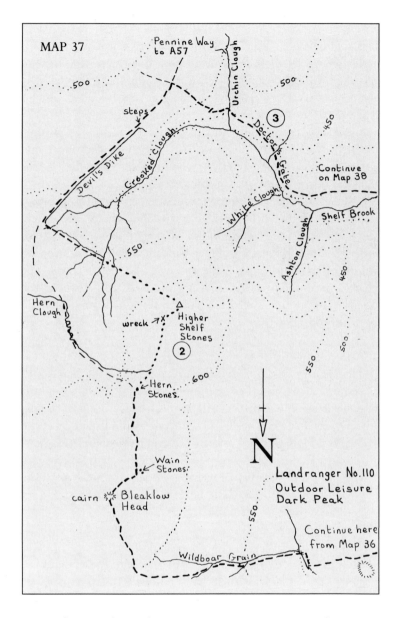

A solitary pole to the SW points to Wain Stones (known as 'The Kiss'), just out of sight but only 200 yards (180 m) away. From here in clear weather Hern Stones will be seen due S less than ½ mile (800 m) distant. The intervening ground is without a clear path although very many feet tread this way every weekend; the reason for this is the peat.

At Hern Stones the Pennine Way is left temporarily in order to visit Higher Shelf Stones (2), the second of the 2000 ft (610 m) summits. This is reached after approximately ½ mile (800 m) on a SW bearing, but by aiming just L of the direct line to Higher Shelf Stones the wreckage of a Flying Fortress aircraft may be visited first.

The escarpment to the SW is Lower Shelf Stones with Glossop beyond, while Shelf Brook flows through the deep valley ahead. Now head SE towards a dyke near the head of Crooked Clough. Climb up this to rejoin the Pennine Way which follows Devil's Dike (probably an old boundary ditch). Turn R and in ½ mile (800 m) a flight of wooden steps is met at the end of a board walk built to minimize erosion. In ¼ mile (400 m) turn R at a crossing path (Doctor's Gate) *(3)* and descend past Urchin Clough to follow Shelf Brook towards Glossop (once known as Glott's Valley).

When the valley flattens out, a further ½ mile (800 m) brings you to the Memorial Footbridge across Shelf Brook. From here the boundary of open country lies ¾ mile (1.2 km) downstream where a track is joined coming in from the R by a barn. Go down this track to cross a stile and over the bridge ahead. The track is now followed through a gap and three gates; the last opens onto an unmetalled road which leads in ½ mile (800 m) back to Old Glossop.

1 Glossop Low Quarries

This quarry, which closed towards the end of the nineteenth century, was used as a source of local building stone, specializing in paving flags and roofing slabs. A rood of roofing slabs was 44 square yards (37 sq m) and cost 52 shillings at the quarry and 64 shillings in the town when the quarry was in its heyday. That the lane which leads up to the quarries on Cock Hill once took substantial traffic is evident from the gritstone paving slabs which may still be seen where they have not yet been covered by encroaching grass.

2 Higher Shelf Stones

This is typical Bleaklow; wild peat groughs (though not as deep as those of Kinder), no path and only the compass to guide you. In bad weather this is quite a frightening place to be; in good weather it is a fascinating area to visit. Bleaklow comes from the Old English meaning 'dark coloured hill'.

Very close to the OS trig point the remains of a Flying Fortress may be seen. The gleaming metal is scattered over a wide area almost as though the accident had only just happened; in fact the crash, in which thirteen American airmen died, occurred on 3 November 1948. Four engines and many metal fragments are scattered about and, although it is illegal to remove any pieces, at one time the entire fuselage and tail could be seen.

The rocks at Higher Shelf Stones are covered more than usual in graffiti, including an early example dating from 7 October 1871.

Old Woman, the view towards Bleaklow

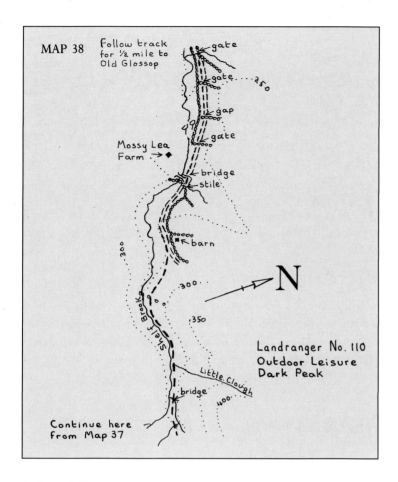

MAP 38 Follow track for ½ mile to Old Glossop

gate

gate ····250

gap

gate

Mossy Lea Farm →◆

← bridge
← stile

← barn

N

Landranger No. 110
Outdoor Leisure
Dark Peak

Shelf Brook

Little Clough

bridge

300
300
350
400

Continue here → from Map 37

3 Doctor's Gate

Gate means road and since 1627 this track has been known as Doctor Talbotes Gate. Dr John Talbot, Vicar of Glossop, 1494-1550, was the illegitimate son of the Earl of Shrewsbury and may have used the old Roman road when visiting his father's castle in Sheffield. The Roman road, from the fort of Navio at Hope to that of Melandra at Glossop, led via Hope Cross, across Blackley Clough, past Hayridge Farm and Oyster Clough to the Snake Road. The next section over Coldharbour Moor, is the best preserved and shows how the road was constructed with slabs set on edge between kerbstones. As the track descends Shelf Brook, it becomes very eroded and loses its character. The road was used by packhorses until the construction of the turnpike in 1821.

CROWDEN BROOK TO RUSHUP EDGE FROM EDALE

STARTING AND FINISHING
POINT
Edale car-park (110-124853).
LENGTH
10 miles (16 km)
ASCENT
1650 ft (500 m)

Crowden Brook makes an interesting way up onto the Kinder plateau, and it is often almost deserted when Grindsbrook is bearing its usual heavy weekend traffic. The strangely eroded stones of the plateau are among the most fascinating of sculptured shapes. The walk encircles the upper Edale Valley which is well seen both from the approach via Upper Booth and from Rushup Edge, a favoured spot for hang-gliders.

ROUTE DESCRIPTION (Maps 39–41)

From the car-park, walk under the railway bridge and up the road towards Edale village *(1)* to the Old Nag's Head which is reached in about ½ mile (800 m). Turn L (PFS 'Upper Booth and Hayfield') to pass through a kissing gate and then over a stile. The sunken track is followed beside a small stream for 300 yards (270 m), and at the PFS ('Hayfield via Upper Booth and Jacob's Ladder') turn L over the stile. Crossing the narrow field, turn R on the far side and walk up the hedgeside to a stile in the corner. Climbing gradually uphill through a series of three stiles, the path flattens out. On the L are the upper reaches of the Edale Valley with Rushup Edge on the far side and Brown Knoll at its head. The prominent notch in the far skyline just to the R of Mam Tor, through which the road to Edale passes, is known as Mam Nick.

The path continues through a further four stiles, descending to turn R at a stile onto an old track. Walk down the track to the hamlet of Upper Booth ('Booth' is the Tudor word for a temporary shelter used by herdsmen). On reaching Upper Booth the track turns L and then immediately R to a stile into the farmyard. Going through the farmyard out onto the road, turn R downhill for a few yards to a bridge. Turn R over the stile

Opposite Rushup Edge from Mam Tor

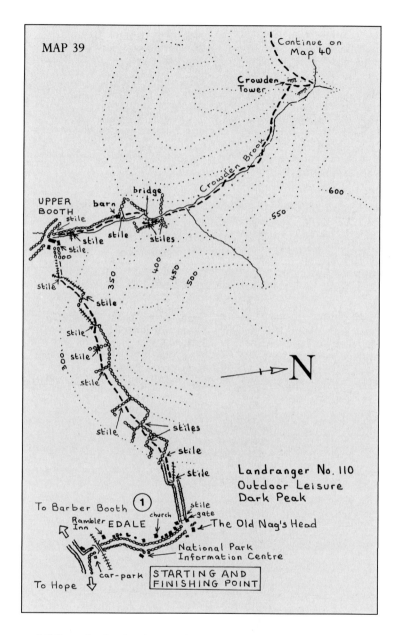

MAP 39

Continue on Map 40

Crowden Tower

Crowden Brook

600

550

UPPER BOOTH
stile
barn
bridge
stile   stile
stiles
stile
stile
350   400   450   500
stile
stile
stile
stile
300
stile
stiles
stile
stile

N

Landranger No. 110
Outdoor Leisure
Dark Peak

To Barber Booth   ①   stile
church   gate
Rambler   EDALE   The Old Nag's Head
Inn
National Park
Information Centre
car-park   STARTING AND
To Hope   FINISHING POINT

and follow the bank of Crowden Brook, crossing a stile and then
up to a barn. Go over the stile and cross Crowden Brook at the
footbridge. Cross another stile, turn L, and at the next stile the
boundary of open country is reached.

The route follows Crowden Brook all the way up to the
Kinder plateau high above, crossing and re-crossing it several
times as the path gradually steepens. When Crowden Tower
looms overhead, climb L to just below the rocks. Turn R and
contour round to join the head of Crowden Brook. The
alternative direct route up the waterfalls is great fun, but only if
you are experienced in rock scrambling.

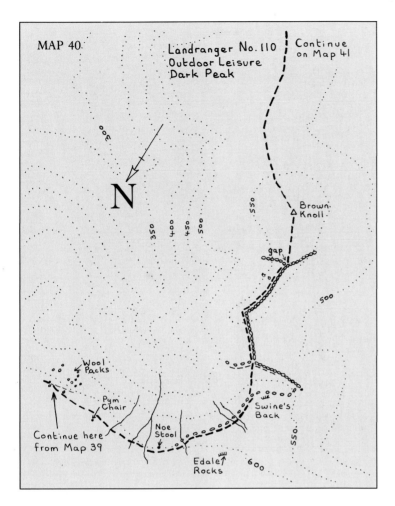

From the head of Crowden Brook, where two streams tumbling down over the bare grit bedrock join, the path turns L to follow the edge. In about ½ mile (800 m), an area of strangely eroded rocks, known as the Wool Packs, is reached. After examining these rocks, which indeed look like bundles of fleeces awaiting collection, head for Pym Chair, the prominent, saddle-shaped rock on the skyline. The path actually skirts Pym Chair, but it makes a good excuse for a stop and a lot of the point of the walk is lost if you hurry past these rocks. The highest point in the Peak District at 2088 ft (636 m) is just north of here. Continue along the wide, and in wet weather boggy, path to Noe Stool, another prominent rock overlooking the headwaters of the River Noe which flows down to join the Derwent near Hathersage. Ahead across the next dip is Swine's Back, a prominent escarpment, and high on the R is Edale Rocks. Following the path beside the broken wall, turn L at Swine's Back and descend to cross the old packhorse route to Hayfield which comes up from Jacob's Ladder on the L. Go up the slope

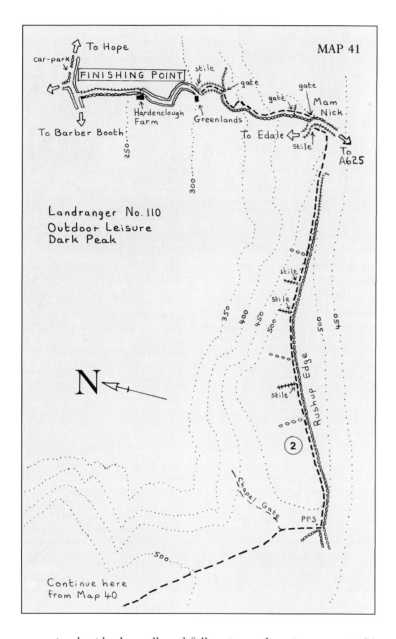

The Wool Packs

opposite, beside the wall, and follow it to where it turns R in ¼ mile (400 m). In another ¼ mile (400 m), at a gap at the junction with a wall coming in from the L, leave the wall and aim SSE towards the unseen OS trig point of Brown Knoll which appears shortly.

Brown Knoll summit to Rushup Edge is about 2 miles (3.2 km) across wild moorland with few landmarks. The general direction to head is SE. A wide path, more or less boggy according to the conditions, will assist, and the air shaft of the 2

mile (3.2 km) long Cowburn railway tunnel provides one useful reference point, until eventually the old Chapel Gate packhorse way is met coming up from Edale on the L (Chapel refers to Chapel en le Frith). Turn R on to this track and in 200 yards (180 m) (PFS) turn L onto the Rushup Edge path. Climb gradually now towards Rushup Edge *(2)*, and ½ mile (800 m) past the PFS a fence is crossed at a stile and the highest point is reached. From here the route is all downhill. Ahead is the Great Ridge, which stretches from Mam Tor to Lose Hill, and in the far distance is Win Hill. The path descends, crossing two stiles, continuing on the ridge to the very end where a sharp L turn leads to a stile at Mam Nick.

Go almost straight across the road to a gate. Follow the wall downhill through a gate, and in ½ mile (800 m) go through another gate onto a fence-lined path which leads to Greenlands, where the road is joined at a stile. In ½ mile (800 m) the metalled farm road comes out on to the main valley road close to the car-park which is just up the road to the R.

1 *Edale Village* See page 75
2 *Rushup Edge*

On the other side of the wall is an ancient trackway, still a right of way, but not often used, which was sensibly constructed out of the wind a few feet down on the lee side to protect the jaggers on this exposed route. Modern walkers, preferring the view, now stick to the crest. Lord's Seat, the highest point, boasts a Bronze Age burial mound, but usually it is the hang gliders which attract one's attention as they soar in the upcurrents of the edge or swoop in low to land.

Away to the R is the large limestone scar of Eldon Hill Quarry. There is a constant battle in the Peak District, as elsewhere, between the preservers of natural beauty and the developers. Eldon Hole, reputedly bottomless, in fact about 250 ft deep (75 m), is a natural pothole on the same hill and the largest open chasm in Derbyshire.

The hummocks and mounds on the slopes facing Edale may look like the spoil heaps of a quarry, but they are in fact the result of landslips, caused by repeated freeze and thaw action on the steep ground. The effect is, of course, most pronounced on this north-facing slope which holds the snow in winter and casts long shadows over the Edale Valley. Farms in the valley will therefore be found on the north side in order to make the best of the sunshine. There is also a marked east-west difference in climate: Jacob's Ladder, at the head of the valley, is very much wetter than the eastern end of the dale, receiving as much as 10 in (254 mm) more each year.

3·23

THE GOYT VALLEY

STARTING AND FINISHING POINT
Car-park on west side of Errwood Reservoir in the Goyt Valley (119-012748).
LENGTH
12 miles (19 km)
ASCENT
1400 ft (430 m)

Before the construction of the Errwood Reservoir, the Goyt Valley was very quiet and peaceful. It is still most attractive, especially when the azalea and rhododendron bushes around Errwood Hall are in bloom; but it is now a very popular place, so much so that on summer Sundays and Bank Holidays a traffic management scheme operates which bans cars from the road in the upper part of the valley. The area is best seen on quieter days, but if you can't, be prepared to start the walk from the car-park adjacent to the Errwood Dam.

Windgather Rocks

143

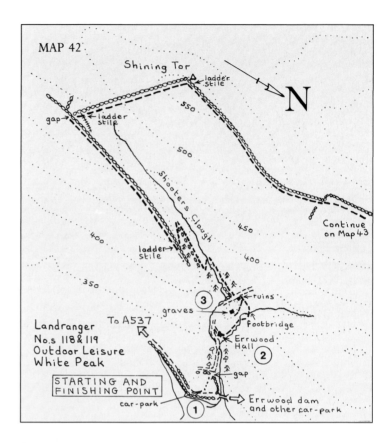

ROUTE DESCRIPTION (Maps 42–44)

Walk up the field behind the car-park above Errwood Reservoir *(1)* to the R gap in the wall (PFS 'Errwood Hall and Trail'). A main path slopes down to the stream and then, as it starts to go uphill again, turn R on the track to Errwood Hall *(2)*. Go in front of the ruins and follow a path through the bushes down to the stream, which is crossed and then re-crossed at a footbridge. Climb out of the clough and up to the ruins of cottages. Here you can ascend the mound on the L, to reach the burial ground *(3)* of the Grimshawe family on top. Return to the ruins and take the waymarked path up Shooters Clough opposite. In 200 yards (180 m) the path zig-zags across the stream to climb gradually up the hill. Another zig-zag in ¼ mile (400 m) leads up to join the path on the ridge at a ladder stile. Turn R, gradually gaining height until in ¾ mile (1.2 km), at the highest point on the ridge, a gap in the wall and a ladder stile beyond lead to a direct approach to Shining Tor.

A ladder stile allows access to the OS trig point (note the grid reference carved on the wall under the stile). Follow the east side of the wall along the ridge, which in 2 miles (3.2 km) brings you to Pym Chair, named after a stone seat now destroyed.

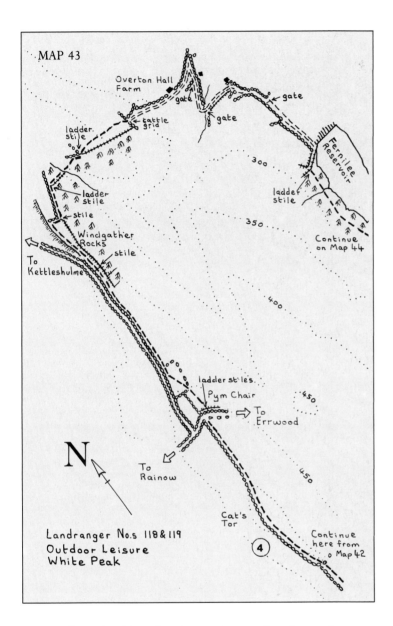

MAP 43

Overton Hall
Farm

gate

gate

gate

cattle
grid

ladder
stile

ladder
stile

Fernilee
Reservoir

300

350

ladder
stile

stile

Continue
on Map 44

Windgather
Rocks

stile

To
Kettleshulme

400

ladder stiles

Pym Chair

450

To
Errwood

N

450

To
Rainow

Landranger No.s 118 & 119
Outdoor Leisure
White Peak

Cat's
Tor

4

Continue
here from
Map 42

Approaching Cat Tor, the shrine *(4)* may be glimpsed among the Scots pine in the valley below to the R. At the Roman road, known as The Street, two ladder stiles lead back onto the moor and a path which soon reaches the road wall. Keep to the R of this wall until Windgather Rocks is reached just after a stile. Walk along the top of the rocks, and then descend to a stile and the wood whose top edge is followed to a ladder stile. Turn R through the wood, up to a wall, and R along this to a ladder stile. Topping the ridge, you can look down into the Goyt Valley. Descend to join a farm road which leads past Overton Hall Farm, and then, becoming a track, doubles back and descends to a gate marked 'Private'. Go through this, and at the

Goyt Forest

stream turn L through another gate and up to a pretty cottage on the L. Turn R and follow the road to Fernilee Reservoir.

At the dam turn R on to the road and then in 150 yards (140 m) go L (PFS 'Errwood Dam') over a ladder stile into the forest. In ½ mile (800 m), at a seat, fork R to a footbridge over a deep clough. The path continues through the woods until it emerges beside the reservoir just below the dam. Crossing the ladder stile, go up to the dam, and turning L cross the slope to the access road on the other side. Climb this to the public road and turn L. Round the corner the road ahead was built on the steep Bunsall incline of the Cromford and High Peak railway *(5)*. Turn R a little way up the hill (PFS 'Goyt's Clough') and follow the path along the hillside and through the trees to Wildmoorstone Brook. The track here used to run down to Goyt Bridge *(6)*, a delightful spot now drowned beneath the water, but the bridge itself has been rebuilt higher up the valley. Turn half L, on to the lower of two tracks, and contour round to an iron girder bridge over the stream. Heading towards the reservoir, turn L beside the wall when the track doubles back. The path follows the wall, first on the L and then on the R, until it turns R down to the stream. Carry on at the same level until the path descends to Goyt Bridge. Turn R on the road beyond, along to the no entry road signs, and then R down some steps to walk beside the river. When the path comes to the road, go straight across onto a track which in ½ mile (800 m) arrives back at the gap in the wall above the car-park.

1 Errwood Reservoir

When the water began to fill Errwood Reservoir on its completion in 1967, drowning the site of the former hamlet at Goyt Bridge, a charming valley was irrevocably changed. Today the scene is different – attractive in a new way; and at weekends small boats beat to and fro on this 78 acre (32 hectare) stretch of open water.

Fernilee Reservoir, built in 1938 is slightly larger than Errwood Reservoir; it has a capacity of 1087 million gallons compared to Errwood's 927 million gallons. Together these reservoirs supply 7–8 million gallons of water daily. Below the Fernilee Dam there is a water treatment works, from which a tunnel under the dam runs to the tower in the reservoir.

2 Errwood Hall

The colourful rhododendrons and azaleas which bloom around the ruins of the hall every spring indicate that it was

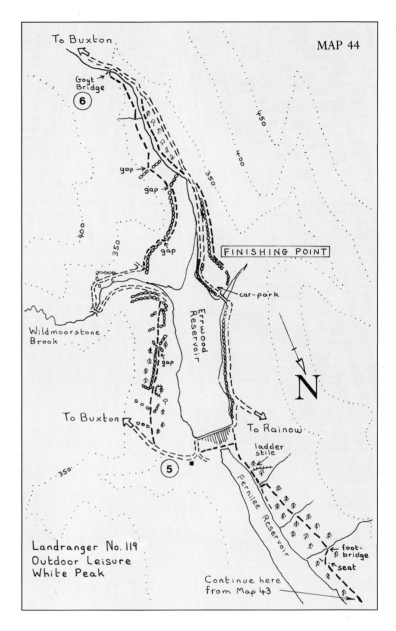

MAP 44

To Buxton

Goyt Bridge

6

gap

gap

gap

350

450

430

400

350

FINISHING POINT

car-park

Erwood Reservoir

Wildmoorstone Brook

gap

N

To Buxton

To Rainow

ladder stile

5

350

Fernilee Reservoir

foot-bridge

seat

Landranger No. 119
Outdoor Leisure
White Peak

Continue here
from Map 43

once a place of some importance. Over 40 000 of these bushes were planted around the house which was built in 1830 by Samuel Grimshawe as a wedding present for his son, Samuel Dominic Grimshawe. The estate employed twenty staff; there was also a private school, servants' cottages, a watermill and a small coal mine. An information board in the car-park shows an engraving of this attractive and delightfully situated hall, as it would once have appeared. One hundred years after it was built, the hall was converted to a youth hostel for a short time before sadly being demolished with the building of Fernilee Reservoir.

3 Burial Ground

On this small hill are the graves of members of the Grimshawe family and some of their servants. It is also the resting place of John Butler who was the captain of the Grimshawe's private yacht the 'Marquita'.

4 Shrine

Restored by the Water Board, this shrine to St Joseph was built in 1889 in memory of Miss Dolores, a beautiful Spanish lady who was companion to old Mrs Grimshawe and who died in her mid-forties on a visit to Lourdes.

5 Cromford and High Peak Railway

This, one of the earliest railways, was completed in 1830 when canals were the usual mode of transport. It connected the Cromford and Peak Forest canals. Steam engines were used to haul the trucks up a total of nine inclined planes connecting level sections of track along which horses were used. The construction owed much to the known art of canal building and followed the contours of the land, with deep cuttings, huge embankments and much sharper curves than is usual for a railway. Inclined planes, the railway equivalent of canal locks, were needed because the track gained nearly 1000 ft (310 m) in height from Cromford. A tunnel, now sealed off, was constructed under Burbage Edge. Although passengers were carried from 1855 to 1877, the service was very unreliable and was discontinued after a fatal accident. As more powerful locomotives became available, the precisely level tracks needed for horses were no longer necessary and better rail routes could be devised which avoided the time-wasting inclines. The line eventually closed in 1892.

6 Goyt Bridge

Now rebuilt by the Water Board about 1 mile (1.6 km) upstream from its original site, Goyt Bridge was on a saltway from Macclesfield to Buxton via The Street, a Roman road. At the time of the Salt Tax it would also have seen smugglers' traffic. The community around the bridge at its old site (now beneath the waters of Fernilee Reservoir) included a private school for about thirty children as well as two farms and two cottages.

3·24

FROGGATT EDGE, BURBAGE EDGE AND PADLEY GORGE

STARTING AND FINISHING
POINT
Hay Wood car-park, near The Grouse
Inn, on the B6054 Calver to Dronfield
road (119-256778).
LENGTH
13 miles (20 km) or 10 miles (16 km)
variant
ASCENT
1150 ft (360 m)

The popular climbing grounds of Froggatt and Curbar Edges are thronged with climbers at weekends. White Edge, which has no cliffs, is quiet by contrast, and has only recently been opened to the public since its acquisition by the Peak Park Board. Longshaw Estate is crossed to Burbage Edge, another popular climbing area, and the walk passes beneath the crags to give a view of the climbs. Higger Tor and the hill fort of Carl Wark are visited, and finally the charmingly wooded Padley Gorge completes this circuit of the edges.

ROUTE DESCRIPTION (Maps 45–48)

Leave the car-park at the far end from the entrance, over the stile and down to the stream. Climbing up to a gate, turn R onto the road and shortly L through a gate at the boundary of open country. Walk along a broad track of silver sand for about ½ mile (800 m) to a kissing gate. In 200 yards (180 m) Stoke Flat Stone Circle is just off the track to the L. The track continues along Froggatt Edge and then Curbar Edge to descend in 1½ miles (2.4 km) to a kissing gate at Curbar Gap.

Turn L on to the road and in 50 yards (45 m), on the R of the entrance to the small car-park, go over the stile by a guide

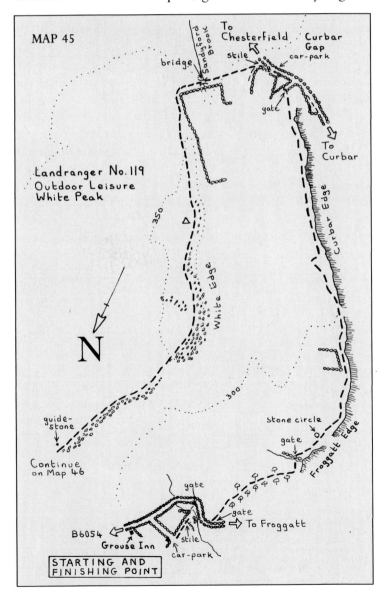

Opposite Froggatt Edge

stone. Go straight ahead, ignoring the L fork, to cross Sandyford Brook at the wooden bridge. Continue beside the wall, which soon bends L, and up onto White Edge. The route is clearly waymarked and in ½ mile (800 m) passes the OS trig point. After 1¼ miles (2 km) the only significant outcrop of rock on the edge is passed. These pock-marked rocks are called Bullet Stones as they were used for target practice during the last war. Go through the wall and across the moor, until a fence is met with White Edge Lodge below on the L. The fence leads down by snow fencing to a stile, and a gate leads you onto the B6054 at a three way junction.

Go straight across the road junction and through the gate by the sign 'Wooden Pole' to follow the main grassy track through the estate and into the wood at a gate. Skirting Longshaw Lodge *(1)*, turn R along the drive to the gate onto the B6521. Go almost straight across to a gate, through the woods for 300 yards (270 m), and then fork R up to the road at a stile. The shorter variant turns L here to the Toad's Mouth.

The wide track opposite leads through a gate and then runs beneath Burbage Rocks for about 1½ miles (2.4 km). At the end go through the gate onto the road, turn L across the bridge and then L again over the stile. In a few yards take the R path which rises gradually and ¾ mile (1·2 km) of easy walking brings you to Higger Tor. Ahead across the dip is the wall flanking the Iron Age hill fort of Carl Wark *(2)*, which is reached by a descent followed by a short ascent. From the old entrance to the fort on

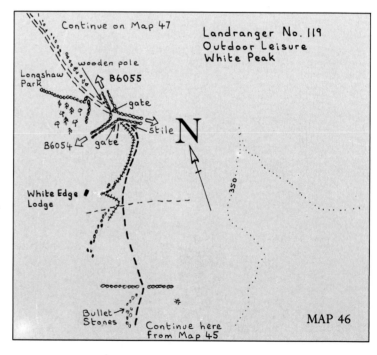

the south-west side, a path descends towards Burbage Brook, but about 100 yards (90 m) before the stream take a small path R which climbs onto the ridge. Follow the rocky ridge down to the road at a stile by the Toad's Mouth Rock, only the eye of which is artificial.

Turn R along the road for a few yards and then L through a little gate into the National Trust estate. Follow Burbage Brook down to meet the woods in about ½ mile (800 m). Just before entering the wood there is a quarry track which leads to a small quarry containing several millstones *(3)* tumbled about among the rocks. Return to follow Burbage Brook as it descends Padley

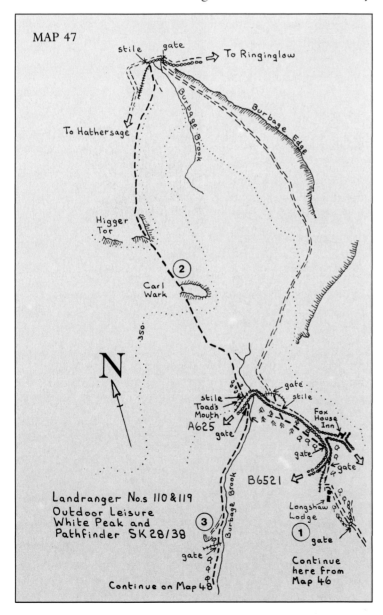

MAP 47

To Ringinglow

stile gate

Burbage Brook

Burbage Edge

To Hathersage

Higger Tor

②

Carl Wark

N

350

gate

stile

stile

Toad's Mouth

Fox House Inn

A625

gate

gate

gate

B6521

Landranger No.s 110 & 119
Outdoor Leisure
White Peak and
Pathfinder SK 28/38

③

Burbage Brook

Longshaw Lodge

① gate

gate

Continue here from Map 46

Continue on Map 48

Gorge, where further millstones may be seen beside the path. Going through a new gate, the path descends gradually for about ½ mile (800 m); when it starts to rise again, don't go L down to the brook, but stay up, and the path soon continues its descent to emerge from the trees in a clearing. Turn R in front of the stone waterworks building and over a stile in the fence to follow a small path through the bracken. The path joins a fence behind the houses and then runs beside a stone wall which soon turns L and descends to the track. The ravine on the R, where the path joins the track, is the Bole Hill quarry incline *(4)*. Turn L on the track beside Padley Chapel *(5)* and walk past the station and over the railway bridge. A path just to the R of the café now leads up to the main road. Go straight across (sign 'No Through Road') and up the hill for 300 yards (270 m) to turn L at the second of the two footpaths. This leads uphill through a gate into a wood and in ¼ mile (400 m) a stile is reached into the car-park.

1 Longshaw Lodge

The 1600 acre (650 hectare) Longshaw Estate belongs to the National Trust. The Lodge was built in 1827 as a shooting lodge for the Duke of Rutland. There is an information centre, shop and cafeteria open from April to the end of October. The sign 'Wooden Pole' at the entrance to the

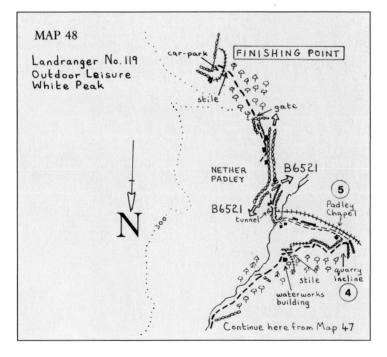

MAP 48

Landranger No. 119
Outdoor Leisure
White Peak

Hathersage Moor

154

estate refers to a guide post on the Dronfield to Tideswell packhorse track. The present post is a recent replacement.

2 *Carl Wark*

This isolated rocky knoll is, like its companion Higger Tor, formed of hard gritstone, the softer surrounding rock having weathered away. It forms a natural defensive position of about 2 acres (0.8 hectares). Fortified on its north side by a 10 ft (3 m) high wall of substantial boulders, it is thought to be an Iron Age hill fort, though some authorities put it later at post-Roman, fifth or sixth century. The original entrance lies at the south-west corner where there is an information plaque and a stone trough.

3 *Millstones* See page 40

4 *Quarry Incline*

Over one million tons of stone, extracted from Bole Hill Quarries, was used in the building of the Derwent and Howden Reservoir dams commenced in 1901. The stone was loaded onto waggons in the quarry, pulled by engines to the top of this incline, and then lowered by gravity under the control of cables which pulled up empty waggons. The incline passed under the track to join the railway, and, as the trucks were standard gauge, they could be transferred directly to the main line.

5 *Padley Chapel*

This Roman Catholic chapel is the private chapel of Padley Hall. When in 1588 two Jesuit priests were found hiding there, they were taken to Derby where they were hung, drawn and quartered. An annual pilgrimage is held here on the last Thursday in July in their memory. After being used as a cowshed, and then to house the navvies who dug Totley railway tunnel, the chapel was rededicated in 1933.

DOVEDALE, THE TISSINGTON TRAIL AND ILAM

STARTING AND FINISHING
POINT
Car-park at the south end of
Dovedale (119-146509).
LENGTH
17 miles (27 km) or 8 miles (13 km)
variant
ASCENT
1200 ft (370 m)

Pickering Tor

Dovedale has been a favourite from the times of Izaak Walton (author of the seventeenth-century fishing classic, *The Compleat Angler*) to the present day. Limestone cliffs and pinnacles thrust up through the trees in a delightful wooded gorge where the path follows the meandering River Dove accompanied by the sound of rippling waterfalls. The Tissington Trail returns the walker to Milldale; and Ilam, beside the River Manifold, marks the end of this long walk.

As the walk is in the form of a figure of eight, with the intersection at Milldale, if you want a shorter walk in Dovedale, turn back to Ilam after Viator's Bridge.

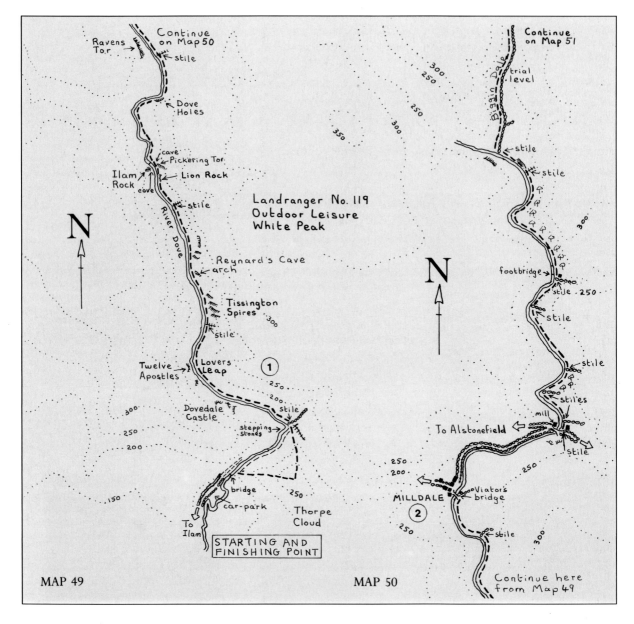

MAP 49

MAP 50

ROUTE DESCRIPTION (Maps 49–53)

Follow the path upstream for 100 yards (90 m) and turn R over the footbridge. Straight ahead is the uncompromisingly steep ascent of Thorpe Cloud, a coral reef knoll. The 500 ft (150 m) ascent can be omitted by following the river upstream to the stepping stones where the route rejoins the river. From the summit rocks, polished like marble from the passage of thousands of feet, there is an excellent bird's eye view of Dovedale *(1)* far below.

Descending directly to the stepping stones, go through the

stile and follow the river round the bend. The broad path leads
to steps which bring you to Lover's Leap, with the pinnacles of
the Twelve Apostles opposite. The path descends to pass
Tissington Spires and then, high on the R, a huge natural arch,
Reynard's Cave. In ½ mile (800 m), Lion Rock (which in profile
resembles a lion) is passed and on turning the corner Ilam Rock
appears on the L, towering above a footbridge. The top of the
stupendously overhanging face is 10 ft (3 m) further out than its
base. Dove Holes, ¼ mile (400 m) further, doesn't live up to its
imposing entrance as the caves are very shallow.

The hamlet of Milldale *(2)* (café and toilets) is reached in
about a mile (1.6 km) at the delightful Viator's Bridge. Stay by
the river following the road for ½ mile (800 m); then cross the
bridge by Lode Mill, an old corn mill, to gain the river's R bank.
Follow the river for 1½ miles (2.4 km) and turn R up Biggin
Dale, which is the second dale on the R. In 1 mile (1.6 km) the
dale forks. Take the R branch (PFS) and in ½ mile (800 m) the
road is reached. Turn L and then, in a few yards, R along a
narrow path beside a house and over a stile. Cross the field to a
stile in the far L-hand corner, and then half L and out over a stile
onto the road. Turn R and continue straight on at the road bend
to follow the track between walls and over a stile. At the next
gate on the L, go over the stile beside it and follow the wall
immediately on the R. Go through the gap ahead and across the
field to a camouflaged stile in the far wall. Turn half R, heading
for the bridge, and cross the gate and stile on the R beyond to
climb up the embankment and onto the old railway.

Turn R on the Tissington Trail *(3)* to Coldeaton Cutting. This
gives way to an embankment with sweeping views on either
side, and in all the railway gives 2½ miles (4 km) of easy
walking. Continue until the bridge (which is almost a tunnel) is
reached. Just beyond, turn R into a car-park and go through this
to the main road.

Go half L and through a stile into the field. Follow the L wall
to the stile at the next road. Turn R and after 150 yards (135 m)
take the stile on the L. The path goes half R up to the wall and
then follows it round high above Dovedale. After two stiles, the
wall is followed down to Viator's Bridge. Go across the bridge,
again into Milldale, and turn L at the road junction by the café.
After 100 yards (90 m) turn L onto a path climbing up the hillside to the first of five fields, which are crossed to emerge onto a
lane. Turn R and then, in 50 yards (45 m) L over a stile. Go half
R across the field to a stile and down into a shallow valley. Turn
L in the valley bottom, cross the stile ahead and immediately go
R over another stile. After a very steep, but short, ascent
continue beside the wall and in ⅓ mile (530 m) above Hall Dale

there is a good view of Dovedale. Now go R up the green lane to a stile and a barn, and continue to a stile at the road.

Go L for ¼ mile (400 m) to a stile on the R just before a house. Straight across to the wall and a stile, then follow the L wall of the field beyond to a stile, and cross the next field to a stile in the middle of the wall. Half R now and down to the gate in the corner by Castern Hall, which dates from the sixteenth century, and follow the main drive down to the road. Turn L to the lodge and go through the garden gate on its L. A fee of 2p per person is payable for the privilege of this route. The often

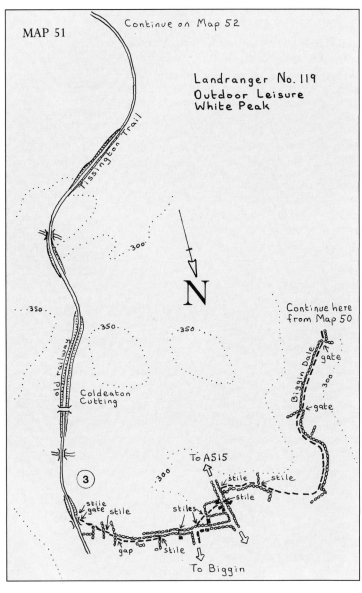

The River Dove near Dove Holes

Viator's Bridge at Milldale

dry river bed on the R is that of the Manifold. The path goes beside this for the next mile (1.6 km), crossing three stiles to Ilam Hall *(4)*. Go round the front of the hall and down the drive to the village of Ilam. At the cross in the centre of the village turn L, and at the bend go through the small gate on the L. Joining a track, go R and through a gate to a small gate beyond. The path follows the hedge towards the Izaak Walton Hotel, then behind it over two stiles. Downhill now and two final stiles bring you to the road opposite the car-park.

1 Dovedale

This is the most famous of all the Peak District dales with the

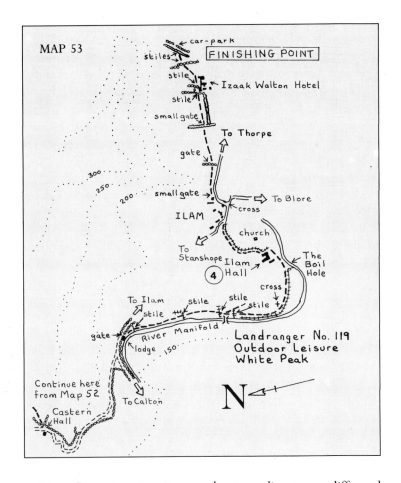

MAP 53

car-park

FINISHING POINT

stiles

stile

Izaak Walton Hotel

stile

small gate

To Thorpe

gate

300

250

200

small gate

To Blore

cross

ILAM

church

To
Stanshope

Ilam
Hall

④

The
Boil
Hole

cross

To Ilam

stile

stile

stile

stile

gate

River Manifold

lodge 150

Landranger No. 119
Outdoor Leisure
White Peak

Continue here
from Map 52

To Calton

Castern
Hall

N

River Dove twisting its way between limestone cliffs and spires in a steep-sided valley. The harder rocks have resisted the erosion process which carved the valley out of the limestone plateau, forming and linking caves into this almost unique environment. Reynard's Cave, distinguished by the remarkable natural arch at its entrance, and Dove Holes, with its large twin entrances, are two of several interesting caves in Dovedale, none of which are very deep. The ash woodland is comparatively recent, most of the trees being less than 150 years old. However, the rocks, each carefully named as the Victorians were wont to do, had begun to disappear beneath the encroaching trees and vegetation until the National Trust, with considerable courage, tackled the problem head on. Many a nature lover must have stood aghast seeing JCBs in Dovedale, but the result is that the famous rocks can now be seen clearly again and the minor disruption can be forgiven. The wide path is a less happy intrusion which hopefully time will heal.

2 *Milldale*

For the fifth edition of *The Compleat Angler* by Izaak Walton, originally published in 1653, an addendum was contributed by his friend, Charles Cotton of Beresford Hall. In this, Viator (the traveller) demurs at crossing this narrow bridge, saying 'Do you travel by wheelbarrows in this country? – tis not two fingers broad'. Since then the parapets have been added. Close by are the remains of an ochre mill which produced the dye from the iron ore mined near Wetton. A millstone lies on the ground by the leat.

3 Tissington Trail

Converted to a grassy track in 1971 from the disused Buxton to Ashbourne railway line, this was one of the first ventures of its kind. The railway was opened in 1899 and although constructed to take a double track, in fact only a single line was laid. Although it carried passengers, its principal use was to convey limestone to the works at Buxton. The line closed in 1967 and the following year the Peak Park Board bought 11½ miles (19 km) of track. The rails and sleepers were removed, five stations demolished and grass seed sown. It now provides a pleasant way for walkers, cyclists and horse riders. One of the features of the trail is Coldeaton Cutting, ¾ mile (1.2 km) long and 60 ft (18 m) deep. The grand bridge high above is only for a farm track. The brickwork of the bridge under the A515 is set in beautiful curves as the bridge is built at an angle to the line to take the road above.

4 Ilam Hall

After a subterranean journey of 6 miles (9.5 km) from Wetton Mill, the River Manifold reappears at the 'Boil Hole' in the grounds of Ilam Hall. The small cave nearby is reputed to have been the home of the hermit, St Bertram. Paradise Walk, the Happy Valley of George Eliot's *Adam Bede*, leads beside the river to a Saxon 'Battle Cross' discovered in the foundations of a cottage during the construction of the model village of Ilam.

Ilam Hall, which probably dates from the sixteenth century, was rebuilt in 1840 in extravagant pseudo-Gothic style by a London businessman, Jesse Watts-Russell, who also reconstructed the village and built the cross in the village centre as a memorial to his wife. In the early 1930s most of the house was demolished and the remaining part, now a Youth Hostel, was saved at the last moment by Sir Robert McDougall who presented it to the National Trust. The church nearby dates from the thirteenth century.

KINDER NORTHERN EDGES

STARTING AND FINISHING
POINT
Car-park on the A57 Sheffield to
Glossop road 6 miles (10 km) east of
Glossop (110-110914).
LENGTH
15½ miles (25 km)
ASCENT
1700 ft (520 m)

Blackden Moor

Kinder's northern edges are often deserted when the area round the Downfall is overrun with groups of walkers. It is not as wild or as uncompromising as Bleaklow and the route finding is much easier, but it is still a place to find solitude and the sweep of moorland under an open sky.

ROUTE DESCRIPTION (Maps 54–58)

On the far side of the road, known as the Snake Pass *(1)*, steps lead down to a ladder stile into the wood. Cross the stream, walk down to join a stream junction and turn L. A forest track is crossed shortly and the stream followed down to a single beam bridge at a bend in the river in about ⅓ mile (540 m). Already the traffic on the busy A57 seems a long way off, although it is only screened by the intervening trees.

Cross the bridge and walk up Ashop Clough where the main track is followed through the wood to emerge opposite Urchin Clough. In ½ mile (800 m), a small pool is passed, and ¼ mile (400 m) later, the ruins of a shooting cabin. The valley begins to widen now and the northern edge of Kinder can be seen high above on the L (assuming the cloud lets you!). After a further 2 miles (3.2 km) and passing Within Clough on the way, the head of Ashop Clough is reached between Mill Hill and Kinder. The Pennine Way is joined at this point (PWS). Turn L and follow it up a steep climb onto Kinder.

At the top of the slope the Pennine Way bears off to the R by a cairn to follow the edge of the plateau round to the Downfall. Strike off ESE towards the highest ground and in about 200 yards (180 m) join a clear path which follows the northern edge overlooking Ashop Clough. Pennine Way walkers setting out on the first stage of their journey are silhouetted on the skyline of Mill Hill. After another 500 yards (450 m) a group of prominent rocks known as the Boxing Gloves will be seen on the L beside the path. The cliffs here are about 60 ft (18 m) high. Continue

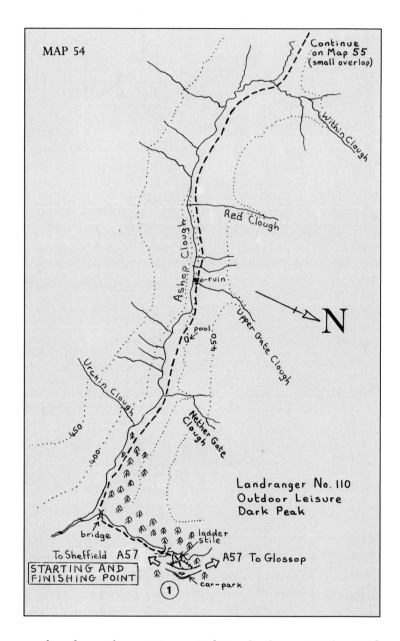

MAP 54

Continue on Map 55 (small overlap)

Within Clough

Red Clough

Ashop Clough

←ruin

N

Upper Gate Clough

pool

450

Urchin Clough

Nether Gate Clough

Landranger No. 110
Outdoor Leisure
Dark Peak

450

400

bridge

ladder stile

To Sheffield A57

A57 To Glossop

STARTING AND FINISHING POINT

① car-park

on the edge path past Upper Red Brook, skirting Nether Red Brook, to reach Fairbrook Naze about 2 miles (3.2 km) along the plateau.

On the very tip of Fairbrook Naze stands a boulder whose supporting plinth is almost worn away, forming an anvil. The edge is now revealed in all its glory stretching away into the distance. Turn R, following the edge path, for about ½ mile (800 m), and then the path bends back on the other side of Fair Brook. Seal Stones is reached next in 1½ miles (2.4 km) where the path turns R, following the edge to Blackden Brook.

The path remains clear for about 1½ miles (2.4 km), passing

Madwoman's Stones which are high above on the R, and then loses its single-minded purpose. If in doubt head E for Crookstone Knoll, which is ⅓ mile (530 m) further, and the path leading to the Knoll should be found again soon. Crookstone Knoll is an excellent viewpoint. To the south is the Great Ridge with Mam Tor and Lose Hill; further round is Win Hill and the Ladybower Reservoir; while to the north are the Woodlands and Alport Valleys.

Turn R, following the edge still, and shortly a quarry is seen on the L. Cut down to join the lower path which is followed downhill to reach a stile. Make for the two sentinel trees and take the L fork down to the wall corner where a track is joined by a stile. Do not cross the stile, but turn L on the track which

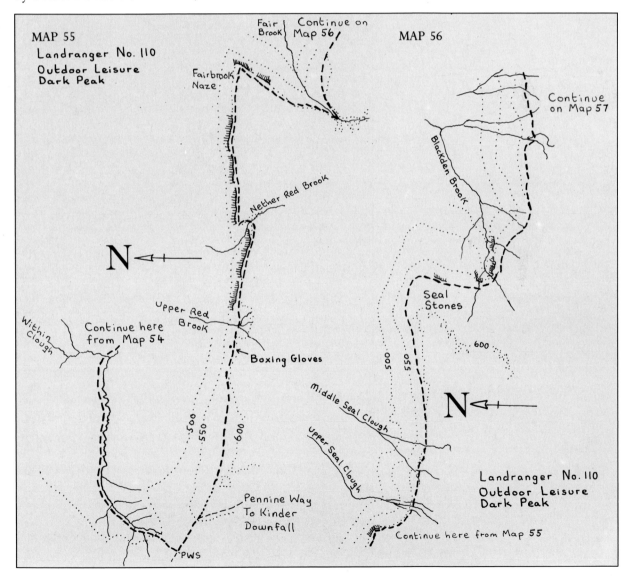

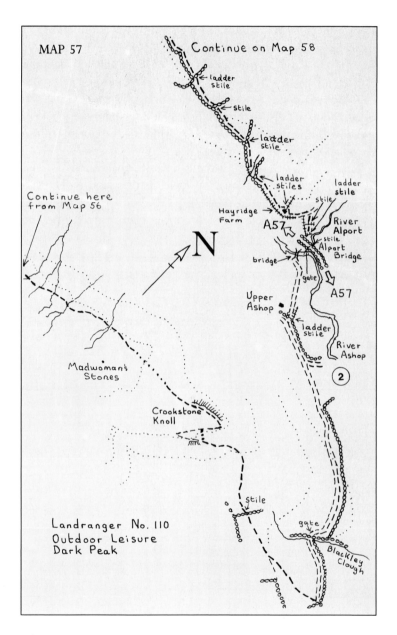

MAP 57

Continue on Map 58

←ladder stile

←stile

←ladder stile

←ladder stiles

ladder stile

stile

Continue here from Map 56

Hayridge Farm →

N

A57

River Alport

stile

Alport Bridge

bridge→

gate

A57

Upper Ashop

ladder stile

River Ashop

②

Madwoman's Stones

Crookstone Knoll

stile

gate

Blackley Clough

Landranger No. 110
Outdoor Leisure
Dark Peak

in ¼ mile (400 m) comes to a gate. Continue on the track, descending gradually until it meets a farm road coming in from the R, and in 1 mile (1.6 km) from the gate reach Upper Ashop Farm.

Just before the farm, turn R over the ladder stile to follow the track down to the River Ashop *(2)* which is crossed at the bridge, or by the ford if the water is low enough. Coming out onto the A57 at the gate, go straight across to the stile. Go over this and two more stiles to the track which leads to Hayridge Farm. Turn L; do not go into the farm, but, just before reaching the gate, strike up the hillside half R to a ladder stile to follow

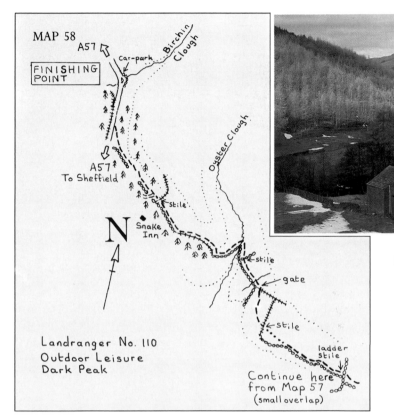

Looking west up the Woodlands Valley

the line of the old Roman road back towards the Snake Inn.

Pass the farm to join a sunken track, which climbs steadily up the hill parallel to the A57; follow it for ¾ mile (1.2 km) over four stiles, and then, after the last ladder stile, the track disappears where the wall turns L. Continue in the same direction to cross the fence at a step stile. The path now reappears and bears R to a gate in the corner of the field. Cross a small stream and go downhill to Oyster Clough, and then, turning L at the stream, climb steeply up the hill to the wood. The edge of the wood continues uphill to the R, but soon levels off thankfully and the path is followed for ¼ mile (400 m) before entering the wood at a stile.

Almost immediately on entering the wood the track bends sharp L through a wall, while a less obvious path goes straight on and this should be followed for ⅓ mile (540 m) until it arrives at the A57. Turn R and the car-park is a short way up the road.

1 Snake Pass

The first sign of winter in the Peak District is usually the announcement that snow has blocked the Snake Pass. This pass, which takes its name from the Snake Inn, is one of the highest turnpike roads in the country, reaching a height of

1680 ft (512 m), and is often blocked in winter, sometimes for many days at a time. Constructed to link the cities of Manchester and Sheffield, it was one of the last roads made by that celebrated road builder, Thomas Telford, and was opened in 1821. Shortly afterwards an inn was built called Lady Clough House after the adjacent clough of that name, but the name was very soon changed to the Snake Inn, in honour of the Duke of Devonshire whose family crest bears a snake. By the time the Snake Pass was built, the railways were already making a great impact on road transport, proving much faster and cheaper, and therefore the pass was never the financial success hoped for by its backers and the trustees were heavily in debt by the middle of the century.

2 *River Ashop*

As one might expect for a mountain region, Kinder is wet—in bad weather, very wet; and with its covering of blanket bog, water is retained for a long time on the plateau. But although the annual rainfall is around 60 in (1524 mm), the wettest part is the Ashop and Alport Valley area in the lee of the high ground. Nevertheless, the River Ashop often seems surprisingly empty in otherwise wet weather. The explanation lies in the engineering works of the Water Board who, seeking to satisfy the thirsty cities, have, with a complex series of weirs and aqueducts, dammed and diverted the waters of both the Ashop and Alport rivers through underground tunnels into the Derwent Reservoir. This work, completed in 1930, was insufficient within fifteen years, so the River Noe also was tapped and tunnelled through the Edale Hills to join the Ashop Valley. In 1960 Peakshole Water and Bradwell Brook were pressed into service, passing through Win Hill to join the Ladybower Reservoir.

The northern edge of Kinder

BLACK HILL

STARTING AND FINISHING
POINT
Crowden car-park on the A628
Woodhead road (110-072992).
LENGTH
17 miles (26.5 km)
ASCENT
2300 ft (700 m)

Black Hill, for many the nadir of their Pennine Way journey north and for some the end of their optimistic hopes and ambitions, has a wild and fascinating charm. The groughs are not as deep as on Kinder, nor is the moor as deserted as some of the secret places on Bleaklow, but in bad weather it can be a tough walk. It is both a wilderness, with black peat bogs that once even threatened to swallow that celebrated guidebook author A. Wainwright, and also a refuge for seekers of quiet places where one may recline on heather and bilberry and gaze at the sky.

ROUTE DESCRIPTION (Maps 59–63)

From the car-park take the path towards the campsite and turn R. At the next junction turn L, go through the gate and then uphill through another. Just before the pine trees on the L, turn R (PFS 'Pennine Way via Laddow Rocks') to follow a fence for ¼ mile (400 m) to a ladder stile. Turn half L up the hillside, zig-zagging through two broken walls to join a wall which leads steeply uphill onto the plateau through tussocky moorland grass. As the angle eases and the wall turns half L, pause for a breather and look back on the northern edge of Bleaklow opposite and Torside Reservoir in Longdendale *(1)* below.

Follow the wall and, when it peters out, continue in the same direction on a clear path to brush the end of another wall. Just after the wall, turn half R, bearing NW, and in less than ½ mile (800 m) Lad's Leap (small cliffs) will be found at the head of Hollins Clough. Cross the stream and turn L to follow the edge of the plateau, which in about ¼ mile (400 m) skirts the top of Millstone Rocks. Leave the path now at a stony area just after the quarry and, turning half L, descend on a grassy, indistinct path for ½ mile (800 m) to Rawkin's Brook.

At the brook turn R along the fence passing (but not crossing) two ladder stiles. After ½ mile (800 m) an old track comes in from the R. Follow this as it descends to pass a disused, dry reservoir on the L. The track now becomes quite wide and is

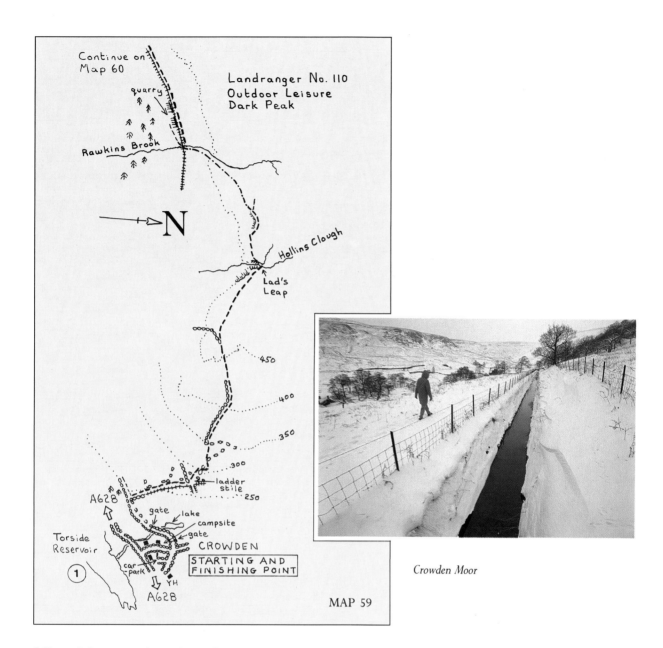

MAP 59

Crowden Moor

followed for 1¼ miles (2 km), through a small plantation by a ladder stile and then through a gate onto the road. Turn R down to the bridge and a few yards up the hill turn R (PFS) and walk up the lane until a ladder stile marks the start of open country again. Turn L over the stile and follow the wall until it zig-zags down to meet the stream in Ogden Clough which is gained via another ladder stile. Cross the stream, climb up the hill for 250 yards (225 m), and turn R onto a narrow grassy path (sign 'Footpath to Chew Valley') which runs parallel to Ogden Clough.

In 1 mile (1.6 km) the path descends to cross the stream at a

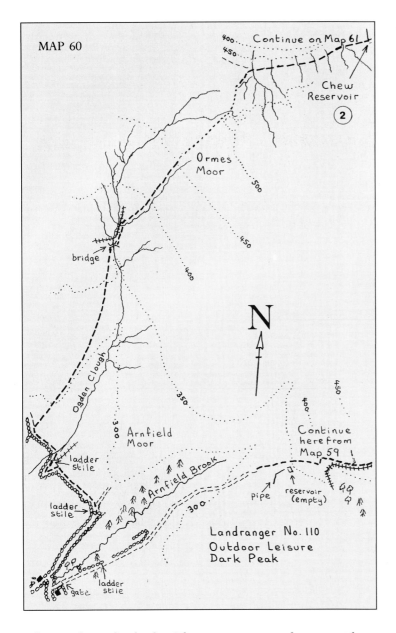

substantial wooden bridge. The stream is crossed again, without the aid of a bridge, and then a side stream, marked by cairns, is used as a guide up to Ormes Moor, heading NE. On reaching the plateau however, all sign of a path is lost and, although a few sorry stakes may pretend some guide, it is better to rely on the compass to lead you NE across the bogs to the rim of the Chew Valley. Turn R along the edge path and walk up to Chew Reservoir *(2)*. In good weather the sight of the tarmac road leading up to the reservoir comes as an unwelcome reminder of

Looking north across Torside Reservoir

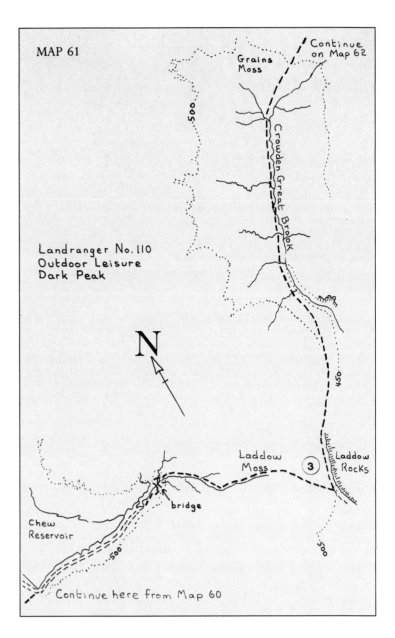

civilization intruding upon the wilderness, but in bad weather the road, glimpsed through swirling mist, is a welcome reassurance that your navigation is correct.

A broad track up the south side of the reservoir leads to a bridge, and then, narrowing to a path, crosses and recrosses the stream all the way up to Laddow Moss, accompanied by frequent large cairns. Continuing on the track as it descends, the top of Laddow Rocks *(3)* is soon reached. It is possible to cut the walk short here by turning R down the valley to the car-park. To proceed to Black Hill however, turn L and walk along the top of the rocks high above Crowden Great Brook (a large

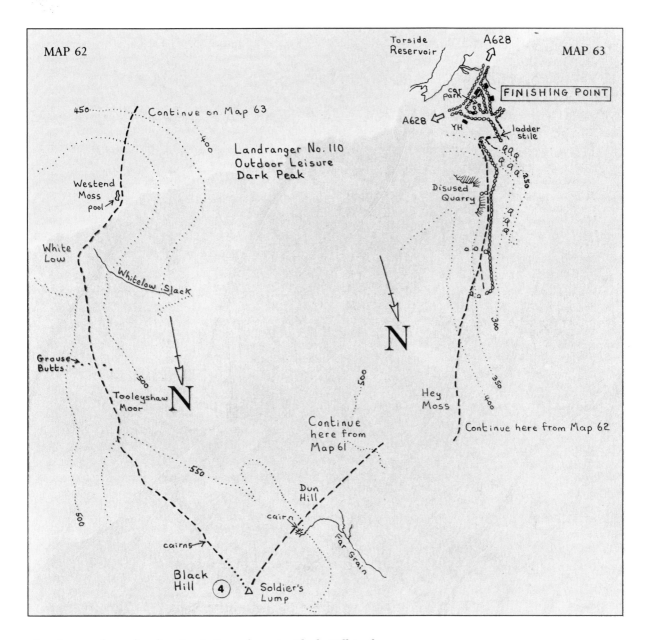

MAP 62

MAP 63

Landranger No. 110
Outdoor Leisure
Dark Peak

clough carved out by the river). From here to Black Hill is the
route of the Pennine Way. The track gradually loses height to
eventually join the stream and 1¼ miles (2 km) after leaving
Laddow Rocks the stream is crossed and then recrossed
immediately at fords. If the stream is in spate this can be
avoided by climbing up the hillside. Continue up the valley,
following the L bank of the stream, and in a further ⅓ mile
(540 m) the stream and path part company. The broad, grassy,
but rather boggy path leads directly up Dun Hill and thence,
heading NW, to a tall cairn. The top of Black Hill *(4)* is only ⅓
mile (540 m) further to the NW.

Arnfield Moor

From the OS trig point there is initially no path, but follow a bearing of 150 degrees and fairly soon a line of cairns is picked up and then a path develops which leads across Tooleyshaw Moor through an area of groughs. The path keeps to the broad ridge bearing S to the top of White Low 1½ miles (2.4 km) from Black Hill and then turns SW to a pool on Westend Moss ¼ mile (400 m) further. From the pool the path goes S to Hey Moss and then begins to descend, heading almost directly for the disused quarries, with Crowden Little Brook far below on the R. Passing a broken wall a more obvious track comes in from the R, and this leads past Loftend Quarry steeply downhill to turn R and over a ladder stile onto the road. Turn L and walk ¼ mile (400 m) back to the car-park.

1 Longdendale

The valley floor is filled for over 4 miles (6.5 km) by a series of five reservoirs, started in 1848, by the engineer John Bateman, with Woodhead in the East, and completed in 1877 with Bottoms in the West. Torside Reservoir is the largest, covering 160 acres (65 hectares), with a capacity of nearly 1500 million gallons and a depth of 84 ft (26 m). The reservoirs, which drowned some mills and dramatically altered the water supply of others, aroused considerable opposition from those affected. However, the needs of Manchester prevailed and the local people, initially fearful of the consequences of a dam failure such as that at Holme in Yorkshire where over eighty people died, found that these dams were trustworthy. At the time they were built this series of reservoirs was the largest such stretch in the world.

The first Woodhead Tunnel, built between 1839 and 1845 to link Manchester and Sheffield, was soon followed by its twin (1847 to 1852). Both tunnels, at the time the longest in the world, continued in use until the third tunnel was completed in 1954. The last train ran through this on 19 July 1981. Largely forgotten, one of the earlier two tunnels was reborn in the 1960s and extensively cleaned and repaired to accommodate the electricity cables of the Central Electricity Generating Board who had received numerous protests at their proposal for an overhead route.

2 Chew Reservoir see page 115

3 Laddow Rocks

This is a popular crag for Manchester climbers, first explored at the turn of this century. An accident here in 1928 so concerned the rescuers about the problems of evacuating a badly injured climber that it led to the formation of the Mountain Rescue Committee and to the design of the Thomas Stretcher by Eustace Thomas, the celebrated fell runner.

4 Black Hill

The summit of Black Hill, known as Soldier's Lump because of its use as a military survey post, was the highest hill in Cheshire until it was demoted by the county boundary revisions. It is still a wild and very remote place requiring skill with map and compass. The OS trig point sits on a little eminence amid a sea of black peat and in wet conditions may not be approachable. Holme Moss television masts, 750 ft (230 m) high and just over a mile (1.6 km) away to the ESE, were built in 1951.

Derwent and Howden Circuit

STARTING AND FINISHING
POINT
Fairholme car-park by the dam of
Derwent Reservoir (110-173893).
LENGTH
21 miles (34 km)
ASCENT
2200 ft (670 m)

This high level circuit of the Derwent Reservoir's watershed covers some of the wildest and most remote moors in the Peak District. It is a tough walk even in good summer weather and should be attempted only by experienced walkers who know how to use map and compass. Try to pick dryish conditions as it is much harder going when the ground is very wet. Usually only a few people will be seen once the high moors have been reached and, with just the grouse and larks for company and rough moorland grass and heather underfoot, the splendid solitude has a very special appeal.

ROUTE DESCRIPTION (Maps 63–70)

From the car-park walk down to beneath the dam and then up the path which doubles back to join the main track beside the Derwent Reservoir *(1)* at a stile. After 1½ miles (2.4 km) easy walking beside the reservoir, and just before the Howden Dam, turn R (PFS 'Bradfield and Strines'). A clear path is followed high on the south side of Abbey Brook (the land belonged to Welbeck Abbey in the twelfth century) and in just under 2 miles (3.2 km) passes Berristers Tor. The path bends R to Sheepfold Clough, where the faint remains of shooting cabins are still just visible. Cross Sheepfold Clough and descend L to cross Abbey Brook. Then, on a faint path which peters out, climb above Foul Clough onto the plateau. Turn L, crossing the upper part of the clough, and follow the edge, where the going is easiest, to Wet Stones, and from here head NW to pick up the clear path which goes N along Howden Edge. The OS trig point on **Margery Hill** is about 1¼ miles (2 km) along the edge, but set back from it and so is easy to miss. From the OS trig point a path leads in ¼ mile (400 m) to cross Cut Gate, the old packhorse route from the Woodlands Valley to Penistone, and from here it is ¾ mile (1.2 km), marked by occasional boundary stakes, to the second OS trig point which is on Outer Edge.

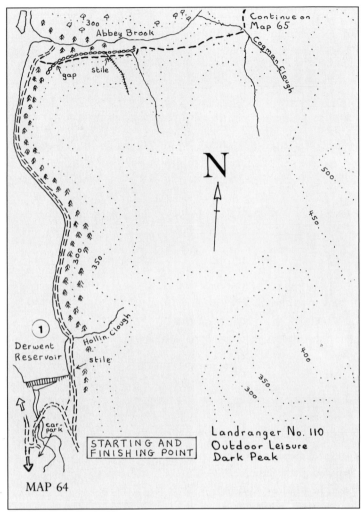

MAP 64

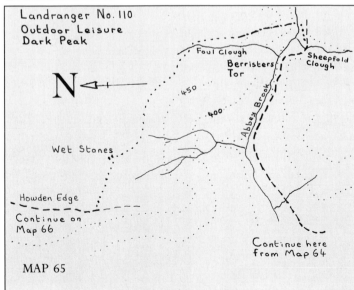

MAP 65

Derwent Reservoir

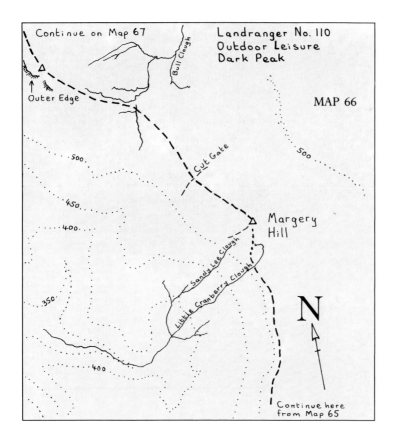

The next 3½ miles (5.5 km) to Swains Head are wild country with few landmarks, but a path has developed in recent years which aids navigation and progress. An isolated gritstone block, with the date 1894 carved on top, is passed just before Swains Head, which is marked only by a small stake and a path which branches off R. Continue for 50 yards (45 m) and then turn L down a clough (no path) to meet the infant River Derwent. Follow this upstream for ⅓ mile (530 m) on a faint path and then climb beside, or in, the clough which leads up onto the plateau (again no path). Continue in the same direction, through the strangely carved rocks of Barrow Stones to the Crown Stone, a very large boulder overlooking the Westend Valley ahead. A path now follows the edge SW to Grinah Stones in ½ mile (800 m) and from here a clear path sets off towards Bleaklow Stones. It is easy to get diverted from the proper route as there are several minor paths, but by taking the upper path if in doubt, Bleaklow Stones is reached in 1 mile (1.6 km).

Go past Bleaklow Stones for about 300 yards (270 m) and then head due S down the ridge (no path). Although there are faint paths over the moor it is easy to lose them, and care is

Margery Hill

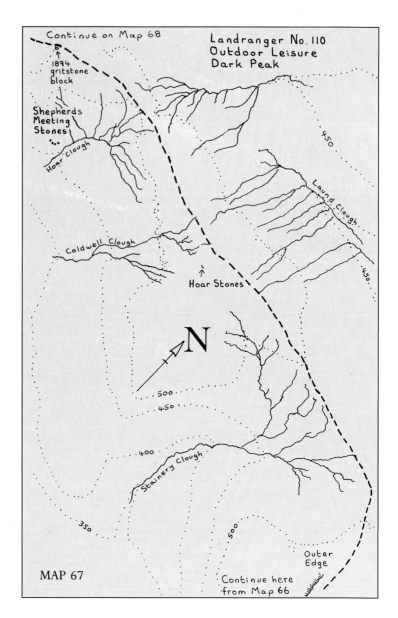

Continue on Map 68

needed to remain on the broad ridge which undulates over a
minor top for over 2 miles (3.2 km) to the OS trig point between
the Westend and Alport Valleys. The path then becomes clearer
and soon gives good views down into the Alport Valley *(2)* on
the R. In 1 mile (1.6 km) a wall is reached and followed to the
cliff edge overlooking Alport Castles. Take care as the drop is
steep and unexpected. The path now gives easy walking for 2
miles (3.2 km) until, as a wall comes in from the R, a ladder stile,
followed shortly by another, brings you out at a major track
junction of a hollowed packhorseway paved with small stones.
Turn L and descend gradually to a gate at Lockerbrook Farm.
Two hundred and fifty yards (225 m) past the farm turn R at a

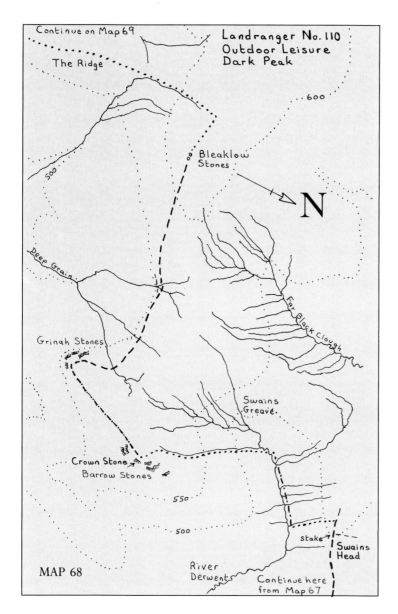

Continue on Map 69

The Ridge

Landranger No. 110
Outdoor Leisure
Dark Peak

600

Bleaklow
Stones

500

N

Deep Grain

Far Black Clough

Grinah Stones

Swains
Greave.

Crown Stone

Barrow Stones

550

500

stake

Swains
Head

MAP 68

River
Derwent

Continue here
from Map 67

gap (PFS 'Forest Walk to Fairholme') and go down to enter the wood at a stile. A path leads down through the trees, over the leat at a bridge, and out onto the road opposite the car-park.

1 Derwent and Howden Reservoirs

The high local annual rainfall, which exceeds 50 in (1270 mm) a year, together with the deep valley which narrows to provide good sites for dams, led to the early exploitation of the Derwent Valley for the benefit of Sheffield, Derby, Leicester and Nottingham. The construction of these masonry dams 115 ft (35 m) high, which taper from 178 ft (54 m) thick at the base to 10 ft (3 m) at the top, was begun in 1901 and

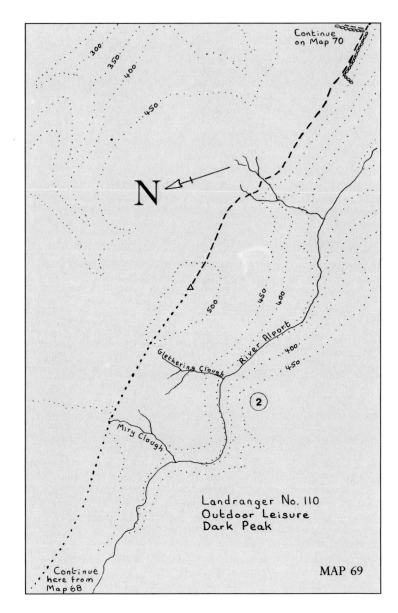

continued for the next fifteen years. Workmen and their families were housed in temporary dwellings which, with school and shops for the thousand inhabitants, became known as 'Tin Town'. The massive amounts of stone for the dams, which were over 1000 ft (300 m) long and built in Gothic style, was quarried at Bole Hill Quarries (see page 000), carried by rail to Bamford and then, via a specially built railway, to Birchinlee on the west side of the valley.

In 1986 a fly past here commemorated the famous Dam Busters who practised over these dams for their epic flight to bomb similar dams in the Ruhr Valley during World War II. The film of their mission was also shot using this location.

2 Alport Valley

The traffic on the busy A57 rushes past the foot of Alport Dale, yet only 5 miles (8 km) up the valley is Grains in the Water, one of the most remote, quiet and, for lovers of solitude, most attractive dale heads in the Peak District. It is seen at its best as you walk back from Bleaklow high on the rim of the deep, steep-sided valley, in the late afternoon sun, or finest of all by moonlight.

Alport Castles, in the lower part of the dale, is a landslip of gigantic proportions where a veritable mountain of gritstone rock has slid towards the valley on its underlying bed of shale.

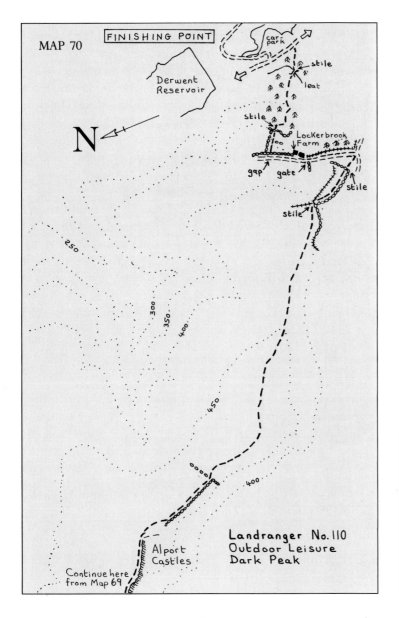

Hagg Farm in the Woodlands Valley

APPENDICES

Access for the Walker

The name National Park is misleading as it is not in fact owned by the nation. Most of the land is in private ownership and right of access only applies to public footpaths or where Access Agreements have been made with the landowners.

The National Parks and Access to the Countryside Act 1949 required the County Council to provide a definitive map showing the public rights-of-way. Inclusion on this map is proof that a right-of-way exists. These are classified as public footpaths or as public bridleways.

There are however other large areas within the Park, known as Access Land, where unrestricted access is permitted.

ACCESS AGREEMENTS

The National Parks and Access to the Countryside Act 1949, as amended by the Countryside Act 1968, makes the Peak Park Joint Planning Board responsible for making arrangements with the landowners for the public to have access to open, uncultivated land, including mountain and moorland. 'Access' means the right to wander at will over the land for open air recreation and is not confined to specific routes. At the present time Access Agreements cover about 76 square miles (19 700 hectares) of open country. It must be remembered, however, that the land remains in private ownership and provides sheep grazing and grouse moorland.

SHOOTING SEASON

Each Access Agreement includes a clause allowing each moor to be closed to public access on up to twelve days each year during the grouse shooting season (12 August–10 December). Lists of dates when the moors will be closed are published monthly for August, September and October. These lists are available from the Board about a fortnight in advance and are also displayed on notices around the area. These notices include a map which shows access moors numbering each shooting area. When specific moors are closed to public access for the day, a sign to this effect is also displayed. There is no shooting on Sundays and hence all access areas are open on Sunday.

THE NATIONAL TRUST

The policy of the National Trust is to give free access at all times to its open spaces; however there cannot be unrestricted access to tenanted farms and to certain ecologically sensitive areas. The National Trust owns land on Kinder and Bleaklow, which are covered by Access Agreements, and also land to the east of the River Derwent, as well as Longshaw Country Park and Lyme Park.

CONCESSIONARY PATHS

There are a number of permissive or concessionary paths in the Peak District. These are marked in red on the Outdoor Leisure maps and are usually signposted and waymarked. Although they are generally open for public use, they are not rights-of-way and the landowner retains the right to close them.

Safety

The walks described in this book cover a very wide range of difficulty, from short, easy strolls which can be completed in virtually any weather conditions at any time of the year, to those which should only be attempted by fit and experienced walkers with considerable knowledge of mountain and moorland navigation.

Despite the lack of really high mountains (only three tops scrape over the height of 2000 ft (610 m) which justifies mountain status), the Peak District provides some very tough challenges. The weather is notorious for its changeability, from good visibility to dense mist, from mild conditions to arctic temperatures, and from a gentle breeze to a strength-sapping gale. Rescuers in the Peak District are called out to about forty incidents each year and, while some are unavoidable, most of these would not have occurred if people had taken sensible precautions.

DO

Ensure you have the right equipment.

Wear boots if there is any rough ground to be covered, for a firm grip.

Take waterproof and windproof clothing.

Take spare warm clothing, especially during the winter.

Carry an ample supply of food with emergency rations saved until the end of the day.

Carry a map and compass and know how to use them.

Obtain a weather forecast before you set out.

Leave word of your intended route with someone, and remember to tell them when you are safely back.

DON'T

Go alone on the high moorland unless you are very experienced.

Leave any member of the party behind on the walk.

Explore old mine shafts and workings.

A booklet *Safety on Mountains* is published by the British Mountaineering Council and is available from Peak District National Park Information Centres or by post from the Peak Park Joint Planning Board.

Giving a Grid Reference

The starting and finishing point of each walk in this book is identified by a six-figure number, called a grid reference, coupled with the number of the appropriate Landranger map. This is a simple way of uniquely identifying any point on an Ordnance Survey map.

Grid lines are the thin lines which run vertically and horizontally across the map at 1 kilometre intervals and are shown on the Land-

ranger (1:50 000). Pathfinder (1:25 000) and Outdoor Leisure (1:25 000) OS maps. Each line is numbered at the edge of the map (and sometimes at intervals across the map as well) with a number in the range 00 to 99. The 00 lines make larger squares with sides of 100 small squares, representing 100 kilometres. These larger squares are identified by two letters. The entire network of lines covering the British Isles, excluding Ireland, is called the National Grid.

The example below shows how to find the grid reference for the OS trig point on the map shown in fig. 3.

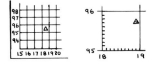

FIGURE 3 *Giving a grid reference*

Step 1

Find the number of the grid line to the *left* of the point. In the example this is 18.

Step 2

Estimate the number of tenths of a square that the point is from this grid line and append this number to the first. In the example this is 9, so now we have 189.

Step 3

Find the number of the grid line *below* the point and append this number to the ones above. Here the number is 95, so we have 18995.

Step 4

Estimate the number of tenths of a square that the point is from this grid line and append this last number. In the example it is 7, so we have 189957. This is called a six-figure grid reference and when the sheet number of the map is also given it identifies a place to within 100 metres.

A full grid reference also includes the identification letters of the appropriate 100 km square of the National Grid.

Countryside Access Charter

YOUR RIGHTS-OF-WAY ARE

Public footpaths – on foot only. Sometimes waymarked in yellow.

Bridleways – on foot, horseback or pedal cycle. Sometimes waymarked in blue.

Byways (usually old roads), most 'Roads Used as Public Paths' and, of course, public roads – all traffic.

Use maps, signs and waymarks. Ordnance Survey Pathfinder and Landranger maps show most public rights-of-way.

ON RIGHTS-OF-WAY YOU CAN

Take a pram, pushchair or wheelchair if practicable.

Take a dog (on a lead or under close control).

Take a short route around an illegal obstruction or remove it sufficiently to get past.

YOU HAVE A RIGHT TO GO FOR RECREATION TO

Public parks and open spaces – on foot.

Most commons near older towns and cities – on foot and sometimes on horseback.

Private land where the owner has a formal agreement with the local authority.

IN ADDITION, BY LOCAL OR ESTABLISHED CUSTOM OR CONSENT, YOU CAN USE, BUT ASK FOR ADVICE IF YOU'RE UNSURE

Many areas of open country like moorland, fell and coastal areas, especially those of the National Trust, and some commons.

Some woods and forests, especially those owned by the Forestry Commission.

Country Parks and picnic sites.

Most beaches.

Canal Towpaths.

Some private paths and tracks. Consent sometimes extends to riding horses and pedal cycles.

FOR YOUR INFORMATION

County councils and London boroughs maintain and record rights-of-way, and register commons.

Obstructions, dangerous animals, harassment and misleading signs on rights-of-way are illegal and you should report them to the county council.
Paths across fields can be ploughed, but must normally be reinstated within two weeks.
Landowners can require you to leave land to which you have no right of access.
Motor vehicles are normally permitted only on roads, byways and some 'Roads Used as Public Paths'.
Follow any local bylaws.

AND, WHEREVER YOU GO, FOLLOW THE COUNTRY CODE
Enjoy the countryside and respect its life and work.

Guard against all risk of fire.
Fasten all gates.
Keep your dog under close control.
Keep to public paths across farmland.
Use gates and stiles to cross fences, hedges and walls.
Leave livestock, crops and machinery alone.
Take your litter home.
Help to keep all water clean.
Protect wildlife, plants and trees.
Take special care on country roads.
Make no unnecessary noise.

This Charter is for practical guidance in England and Wales only. It was prepared by the Countryside Commission.

Addresses of Useful Organizations

British Mountaineering Council,
Crawford House,
Booth Street East,
Manchester, M13 9R2

Addresses of hill-walking clubs available on enclosure of a stamped, addressed envelope.

The Camping and Caravanning Club
11 Lower Grosvenor Place,
London, SW1W 0EY
01-828 1012

Council for National Parks,
45 Shelton Street,
London, WC2H 9HJ
01-235 0901

Countryside Commission,
John Dower House,
Crescent Place,
Cheltenham,
Gloucestershire, GL50 3RA,
Cheltenham (0242) 521381

The Long Distance Walkers Association
Kevin Uzzell – Membership Secretary,
7 Ford Drive,
Yarnfield,
Stone,
Staffordshire ST15 0RP
Stafford (0785) 7606 84

Losehill Hall,
Peak National Park Study Centre,
Castleton,
Derbyshire, S30 2WB
Hope Valley (0433) 20373

The National Trust,
36 Queen Anne's Gate,
London, SW1H 9AS.
01-222 9251

The National Trust
(Regional Office for the Peak District)
East Midlands Regional Office,
Clumber Park Stableyard,
Worksop, S80 3BE
Worksop (0909) 486411

Nature Conservancy Council,
Riversdale House,
Dale Road North,
Darley Dale,
Matlock, DE4 2HX
Matlock (0629) 734343

Peak District National Park,
Aldern House,
Baslow Road,
Bakewell,
Derbyshire, DE4 1AE
Bakewell (062981) 4321

Peak Park Conservation Volunteers,
As for Peak District National Park above
(Ext. 339).

Ramblers' Association,
1/5 Wandsworth Road,
London, SW8 2LJ
01-582 6878

Youth Hostels Association (England and Wales),
Trevelyan House,
8 St Stephens Hill,
St Albans,
Hertfordshire, AL1 2DY
St Albans (0727) 55215

INDEX

Place names and sites of interest only are included. Page numbers in *italics* refer to illustrations.